Try Softer

How to recover your natural state of happiness and clarity of purpose

by

Thomas A. Newnam

International Standard Book Number 13: 978-1-60452-145-0
International Standard Book Number 10: 1-60452-145-7
Library of Congress Control Number: 2019946581

BluewaterPress LLC
2922 Bella Flore Ter
New Smyrna Beach FL 32168

This book may be purchased online at -
www.bluewaterpress.com

DEDICATION

To my grandchildren: Isabeau, Olivia, Kael and Tate

"How to fail: Try too hard."

Malcolm Forbes

AUTHOR'S NOTE

While all circumstances and events in the book are true, revealing relevant aspects of my life up to the age of 70, readers may consider it slightly modified in the following ways:

(1) Out of respect for their privacy, I have changed the names of some of the people, and also left out personal details of their life that do not promote the book's primary focus.

(2) Except for letters, and cases where I was able to record conversations, portions of the dialogue may be considered paraphrased versions of real conversations. I did my best to stay true to the words actually spoken. The many coincidences and synchronistic moments throughout the book actually happened as described.

Graphics: The balance graph and cartoons were created by the author to illustrate how counter productive trying too hard can be. But they wouldn't have looked professional enough to use without the help of Brian Peters and Shashwat Mishra.

Balance Graph – page 159
Cartoons – Pages 29, 42, 55, 69, 112, 247
Photos – Pages 117, 205, 208, 213, 216, 230

CONTENTS

Foreword

"Push through it!"
        "Limits are just an illusion!"
        "No pain, no gain!"
"Try harder!"

In our competitive, success-driven society, at one time or another most of us have come in contact with these statements, which are ego-driven motivators intended to stretch us beyond our current limits, to become more, achieve more, accumulate more. From an external perspective, there is never enough of "more," whereas from an internal perspective there exists within us an inherent capacity to cultivate the soul-stretching qualities of more courage, more love, more wisdom, more mindfulness, more clarity of heart, more compassion for oneself and others. And this is precisely why Thomas Newnam's *Try Softer* is a trustworthy companion as we walk through the challenges and graces of life on the pathway to freedom and joy.

When we "try softer," we no longer rely on the inner critic's berating mind chatter to motivate us. Instead, we allow self-acceptance, self-trust, and self-compassion to be livable, practical, governing principles and practices in our lives. We learn to nonjudgmentally allow the unfolding of our moment-to-moment experiences in all of our life structures. Even in the midst of pressure, stress, distractions and heartaches, we can confidently practice Tom's teaching of loving self-allowance that invites us to mindfully accept what is happening in the present moment, bringing to mind Buddhist teacher Sylvia Boorstein's mantra: "May I meet this moment fully; may I meet it as a friend."

Without a deep understanding of the potential of the human heart — the self-compassion and self-allowance described in this book — we will continue living under the spell of societal conditioning and the magical thinking that if we just push hard enough, repeat our affirmations convincingly enough, we will break through any and all limitations and manifest our material desires and heart's longings. And if we don't, then we are shamefully, sadly, at fault.

Because so few people have a conscious practice of self-compassion, they are not aware of the proven power of being kind to themselves. Many individuals confuse self-compassion with having a pity party and therefore cannot ameliorate their suffering through self-kindness. Throughout this book, Tom's descriptions of the case histories of persons with whom he's worked, combined with the various practices he offers, enable us to uproot that misconception. He also frees us from the myth of perfection, for certainly if we were perfect, we wouldn't be human. By being reminded that our humanness includes life's paradoxes — sadness balanced with joy, gain with loss, shadow with light — we lighten up on ourselves. He reveals the healing power of self-kindness and self-compassion, both of which are so needed in navigating the human experience. By giving ourselves these gifts, we loosen our tight grip on self-judgment and in its place discover that the human heart is expansive and limitless, encouraging us to cultivate its inherent capacities.

"Trying softer," as Newnam defines for us, "means trusting the Universe to bring you home to your heart." The heart is a very wise organ, and by attuning ourselves to its intuitive intelligence, we begin to recognize that there is an overarching grace that is ever available to us, which in turn builds our trust in the fundamental goodness of the universe. As Carl Jung so aptly describes in *Psychology and Alchemy* (*Collected Works of C.G. Jung Volume 12*), "It is conceivable that by intense effort a person may catch a fleeting glimpse of his own wholeness, accompanied by the feeling of grace, which always characterizes this experience." By trusting in this grace, we can directly experience how trying softer opens us to an inner space where we are able to recognize the tangible action of grace upon our life. Suddenly, there is light at the end of the tunnel, a luminosity shines on our path that makes the crooked places straight, and a realization occurs that by being open to the presence of grace we become receptive to the fullness of its gifts, which are offered to us in every moment. The questions become: Do we consider ourselves worthy of receiving them? Will we allow grace entry into our tabernacle of being to deliver its insights and blessings?

The book you hold in your hands is an authentically transformative invitation to awaken you to the sublime beauty of your heart and the gifts of your soul that are the birthright of all beings. Tom's own personal journey, and those of his clients, students and teachers alike, illuminate the path to reclaiming our inherent wholeness, radiance of being, and awakened nature. May its teachings nourish and bless your heart.

Michael Bernard Beckwith
Author of Spiritual Liberation and Life Visioning

Pivotal Validation

Because this book flowed more through me than from me, throughout the writing process I felt more like a scribe than an author. The words came so effortlessly that the moment I decided I had it in acceptable first draft form, in order to validate what I thought (certainly hoped) was the case — that I had created a truly solid and helpful manuscript — I experienced an urgent need to gain an honest, educated and objective opinion of the content.

Though I felt a little nervous to even ask them, not wanting to impose, I felt the most qualified people in my life at the time to both fully understand and objectively evaluate my manuscript were Lew and Janet Klein. They are two of the most prominent names in media outlets across the world. Both are universally respected educators recognized for the many selfless ways they have dedicated their lives to helping others, especially in the area of television broadcasting. I've included a condensed bio about Lew and Janet on one of the last pages of this book.

In response to my request, after reading my manuscript, these two most inspirational people, mentors to so many, graciously composed the following message of official praise. They wrote it together, signed it together and sent it to me happily and without reservation. I felt honored and deeply grateful. Upon receipt of their evaluation of my text, I felt a warm wave of validation.

You will learn more about what role these two beautiful humanitarians have played in my life as you journey through these chapters.

Here is the combined endorsement I received from the Kleins:

Tom Newnam, as a trained family counselor and therapist, saw the firsthand need to help people recognize their personal problems and limitations and reach satisfactory conclusions.

In his soul-searching book, *Try Softer*, Tom points out the need to pause before making choices, just as Robert Frost in his poem "The Road Not Taken" tells how, at a crossroad, he selected the less trodden road knowing he could not come back to travel the other road. And "Oh the difference."

There are decisive times in everyone's life when choices must be made that dramatically determine the direction of one's future. There are occasions when achievement is accomplished only through necessary physical and emotional effort. And there are times when the inner soul, in its honesty, tells one to relax, hear God, and "Try Softer."

Tom reveals the inner wisdom of taking a softer approach, not based on ego satisfaction but in consideration of happiness, love, and contentment. He offers gentle and clear reassurances that although each of us has challenges and fears, we must first reach an intimate and personal understanding of our own self.

In his book, Tom Newnam focuses on "Self Appreciation," offering an upbeat list he titles "Dancing With Your Higher Self." He then presents case studies, including his own experiences, each of which provides a story that represents the wisdom of "Trying Softer." Tom's writing soothes the emotions and satisfies the intellect of the reader. He offers sound guidance to help you find the strength and faith to communicate kindness and love to others. The healthiest path to reaching your own goals is one of authenticity and spiritual alignment. Such a journey, most sacred and personal, will lead you to the kind of happiness and joy that everyone cherishes.

Prologue

In 1980 I was impressed by a Zen parable. Its author is unknown. I discovered it in a book by Joe Hyams, entitled *Zen in the Martial Arts*. As a dedicated karate student at the time, I absorbed the wisdom of the entire book. But it was the powerful lesson in this short parable you're about to read that affected me the most.

In a moment of deep insight, I understood that the story teaches more than just a way to understand karate training. It teaches a most fundamental, valuable, and practical lesson of self-mastery, upon which everyone's happiness depends.

Welcome to my book. Inside you will find inspirational stories about me as well as others who, by meeting various challenges, have finally learned, sometimes the hard way, to "Try Softer" each day. Composed of words from my heart, each chapter includes offerings of wisdom, insight and practical keys for growth.

This book landed in your hands for a reason. I trust it will find its way into your heart as well. I believe that no matter what's going on in your life today, the "Try Softer" approach to living will help you discover the secret to unblock your happiness. The coolest thing you are going to find out is that all you need to do is stop trying so hard.

At the beginning of your journey through my book, I would like to share with you the same, most valuable and thought-provoking, parable that was told to me on the first day I entered karate class. My hope is that you will find this story, commonly shared among martial arts practitioners, to be a bedrock guide and helpful reminder to choose to stay balanced and in the present moment as often as you can. When I started karate training as a white belt, it was drilled into me to honor this teaching tale, to memorize it and to live by it. Years later, when I became a black-belt instructor myself, it was my favorite lesson to teach my students.

I offer the following parable to you — the author of which is unknown — trusting you will be able to give yourself the gift of absorbing and applying one of the best life lessons ever learned in any martial arts dojo. This traditionally taught life lesson has helped me, and generations of countless other martial artists, to walk a more focused and balanced life path. May it soulfully serve you as well.

Karate Parable

A young Japanese boy once travelled, far and alone, across his country to the most respected karate school he'd ever heard of.

Upon arrival, he was welcomed by the famous head sensei of the institution.

"Why is it you have come to our dojo?" the sensei asked the boy.

"I wish to be your student and become the finest karateka in the land," the boy replied. "How long must I study with you?"

"Ten years at least," the sensei answered.

"Ten years is a long time," said the boy. "What if I studied twice as hard as the other students?"

"Twenty years," replied the sensei.

"Twenty years!" What if I practiced day and night with all my effort? Did nothing else but work out?"

"Thirty years," was the sensei's response.

"Why is it that each time I say I will work harder, you tell me it will take longer?" the confused boy asked.

"The answer is clear," replied the gentle sensei. "When one eye is fixed upon your destination, you have only one eye left with which to find the Way."

Chapter 1

The Power of Love

"Trying Softer" means allowing your heart to guide you, rather than your ego.

As a psychotherapist, I've counseled many people suffering from various forms of distress after traumas, commonly referred to as PTSD. One particular, most inspirational, woman comes to mind. She was 90 when we met. I was already a couple of years into retirement.

One morning I received a frantic phone call from a friend of mine. She was so upset I could hardly understand her.

"Tom, can you please come and help my mother! She is crying and choking and screaming. She was raped when she was little, and she still relives it sometimes. She's reliving that right now! Please hurry! I think she's having a psychotic episode!"

Thankfully, I lived only a couple of miles away. I jumped into the car and sped toward her home. I wondered to myself why I didn't feel scared or worried. I should have been, because I had no idea what to expect. What could I do if she was psychotic? I couldn't even imagine how I was going to help.

As I would learn in greater detail later, Helen had been sexually assaulted. One sunny afternoon, a demented farm hand, whom little Helen had totally trusted, lured her into an old shed. When the child entered the darkened room, the man overpowered her. He slammed her to the concrete. Thud! Then he took his pants down and sat on the little girl's chest. He proceeded to sodomize her. In that act of unspeakable violence, he robbed little Helen of her precious innocence. She was five.

Within minutes I arrived at Helen's home. Even before entering the front door, I could hear Helen inside crying. Her daughter let me in and quickly led me down a hallway. We entered her mother's bedroom. Because I had never met Helen before, I knew she would panic even more upon seeing a strange man entering her bedroom. But I didn't have time to worry about that. I just had to do whatever I could to help her.

The dear woman was as distressed as anyone I'd ever been around. Half-sitting on and half falling off her chair, she kept heaving her upper body back and forth in a strained rocking motion. It was obvious she was reliving the attack. Her utterances of pain were primal and gut-wrenching. She kept gagging and choking. When she saw me, she screamed louder and began spitting. I froze in my tracks. Then I did the softest thing I could think of to do; I turned everything over to God.

The next thing I knew, I had dropped to my knees in front of Helen.

"Should we call 911?" her daughter asked frantically.

I wanted to say yes. I even tried to. But I couldn't speak. Helen began to choke uncontrollably. She was spitting, coughing and gagging. She was in an awful state. I thought she was going to die.

In an instant, I felt absolute peace. Still on my knees, I moved as close to the gagging woman as I could. I allowed my arms to rise upward and wrap caringly around her slowly. At first, she squirmed as if she wanted to break free of my embrace.

I kept praying for God's guidance. Within seconds, I could feel the love flowing through me and into Helen's whole being.

Holding her gently, I kept speaking to her reassuringly. I softly patted and rubbed her back. I whispered soothing affirmations in her ear. The words came more through me than from me. Soon I could feel this frightened woman hugging me back. What a beautiful moment and breakthrough that was.

Phew-w-w. Thank God, I thought to myself. "No need to call 911," I said.

I kept assuring Helen that she was safe. She began to sob. When I thought the time was right, I reminded her where she was, and that her daughter was here with us. Gradually, Helen began to re-enter the present moment. I was careful not to encourage her from one state of consciousness to another, too fast. Soon she calmed down and began to compose herself. Then she opened her eyes and looked directly at me. That's when tears began to flow from my eyes.

"I'm so sorry. I'm so-o-o sorry," she said. "I am so ashamed. So ashamed."

I reassured her that there was no need to feel any embarrassment. I told her how deeply honored I felt, and how inspired I was by her openness and courage. "You are an inspiration to me, Helen," I said. "I need to thank you."

She hugged me tenderly, like my own mother. Then she slowly raised herself up from her chair. Smiling, she said: "You'll never know how much you helped me. Thank you. Now I need to freshen up." She headed toward the bathroom.

"That was amazing!" the woman's daughter said. "How did you do that?"

"I don't know!" I said. "I didn't do anything. I just allowed love to flow. I felt only peace."

When Helen reentered the room, her eyes were bright. Her face looked surprisingly fresh. She had even put on lipstick. She smiled and thanked me again. I knew she was going to be okay.

"Now, can I fix you two something to eat?" She hugged her relieved daughter.

When you "Try Softer," you allow love to flow unconditionally.

Suffering for eight decades with PTSD after unspeakable abuse, this beautiful woman had convinced herself she was unlovable. That's what children do when they are abused, especially when they've been betrayed by the people they most trust and depend on. Thank God I was unblocked enough to *allow* God's love to pour from my heart to Helen's. No strategy or clever counseling technique I might have used that day could have opened her up the way love did. All I did was to allow *"Soft Power"* to flow through me.

Love is the only true power in the Universe.

After that day, I started bringing Helen flowers every few weeks. That was three years ago. She hasn't had such a dissociated episode since. Many of the cards she sends me include a handwritten poem. She always signs: "Forever Friends."

The journey to a better life begins with deeper self-acceptance. This means accepting everything about yourself, without judgment. To the extent you can accept the truth of *all that you are,* the barriers to your dreams will dissolve. By the time you embrace your total self, you won't need them anymore. Self-love will flow through you, keeping you vibrantly happy and healthy. And the pain of self-condemnation will be lifted.

A wise (unknown) physician once said, "The best medicine for humans is love."

Someone asked: "If it doesn't work?"

He smiled and answered: "Increase the dose."

Unblocking the Flow

As you will discover, this book is filled with many more true and inspiring stories about one person or another trying to get love flowing.

I chose this chapter to be the first in the book because its title says it all. Love *is* the only real power in the universe. As your journey into subsequent chapters continues, pay attention to how each person struggles to allow love to flow. That's really what we all try to do, all the time.

Chapter 2

The Silent Song

"Trying Softer" means respecting the dignity and rights of others while focusing on your own need to change.

"Open your mouth, dammit!!" The rough, red-faced father screamed at his teenage daughter as he tried to ram a hot dog down her throat.

I couldn't believe what I was witnessing! Ever since the family had sat down to lunch about 15 minutes prior, I'd witnessed nothing but drama. The parents kept crying, pleading and commanding their daughter to eat something. It was obvious they were desperate to get her to take a bite of her sandwich. What was even more apparent was that the girl had no intention of putting anything in her mouth. It was a very upsetting scene.

While the husband kept trying to, literally, pry their little girl's jaws apart, his wife sat like a statue, frozen in her chair. Her hands seemed plastered to her own mouth. She obviously felt helpless watching the two people she loved most battle for control.

Though I had been in situations before with parents and children fighting, in this case, I felt no pressure to intervene. Nor was I worried about getting splashed by flying mustard. The reason I knew I wouldn't be directly affected was because all the while this drama was unfolding, I was seated comfortably in the classroom of a teaching hospital. I was observing the whole thing on a computer monitor.

Along with my professor and two fellow graduate students, I was studying a real-life family therapy training film. It was comforting to know that the session was being directed by a highly competent therapist in a hospital setting. With the family's written permission, this powerful video had been offered to us, as a teaching tool. Such real-life training tapes were invaluable on our paths to becoming certified family therapists.

At that time, as a juvenile probation officer, I was part of a three-person, mobile family-therapy unit. Our purpose was to take therapy to families in our community who couldn't get to a counseling office. It was an innovative kind of "Have Therapy–Will Travel" trial program. Over time, it proved quite successful. I fully appreciated the intimacy and personal privilege of helping people in their homes.

Case Background

Though these parents had a history of various issues with their daughter, it took a life-or-death situation to finally get them into family therapy. Their 15-year-old daughter was suffering from Anorexia Nervosa. For many months leading up to this critical point, every time the frail teen got on the scales, the numbers decreased. Each day the battle to get their child to eat something—anything—was becoming more and more exhausting for the parents. Occasionally, she might eat a tiny morsel, but only enough to keep herself alive. Beyond that, no amount of reasoning, begging, coaxing, cajoling, demanding or bribing had worked to get her to take care of herself. Neither had medication or individual counseling been successful enough to inspire the girl to start eating again.

For the preceding few days of this therapy session, she had refused to eat anything. She was big boned for her age, and down to around 65 pounds. She barely had the strength to stand. It was at this critical juncture when the parents finally agreed to participate in a series of family-therapy sessions at a prestigious children's hospital in Philadelphia. Whether they had heard that family therapy is often the best way to cure certain kinds of eating disorders, I don't know. But clearly, by this time, both parents were willing to do anything to save their child's life.

How I felt watching the session

In addition to studying tapes of excellent therapists working with all kinds of families, the heart of our training involved each of us working with our own caseload of real-life families. We learned the most from those highly supervised clinical sessions. Even though I knew what it was like to work face-to-face with people, watching this heart-wrenching battle for control viscerally affected me. I felt as if I was in the room with them. It was that powerful.

I'm sure part of the reason I was so affected was because I had a daughter of my own. Though my little girl was perfectly healthy, I couldn't help but identify with the parents' desperate attempts to stop their daughter's self-destructive behavior. What loving parent wouldn't try to do that? I felt that I wanted her to eat every bit as much as her father did.

At the same time, another part of me kept rooting for her to stand her ground. That part of me didn't want her to give in to such an assault on her personhood, no matter how lovingly motivated it was.

As I watched the struggle between the father and daughter (which I knew the therapist was prepared to stop at the right time) something about witnessing a stronger person trying to get a weaker person to do something she didn't want to — or couldn't — do triggered in me a strong sense of injustice. At the same time, I couldn't blame either parent for doing exactly what they were doing. For all I know, I might have handled it the same way if I were in such a desperate father's shoes. It was gut-wrenching for me to watch these parents relentlessly pursue the only course of action they thought could save their little girl's life. They were on the wrong track, doing more harm than good. But they didn't know it. They were coming from love.

It was obvious to me that this young girl was not going to see her sixteenth birthday *unless* her parents stopped trying so hard. But the child wasn't just being stubborn. She was fighting for the dignity and right to control her own body. Somehow, even beyond that, I felt she was taking a stand for every human being to have the right to their own personhood.

God bless these loving parents, I thought. They were apparently caught in a Catch-22. Can you imagine? They knew if they didn't do something, and soon, their daughter was going to die. Yet the harder they tried to change her behavior, the more she resisted. It's like those Japanese handcuffs we used to get as kids: you put your fingers in them, and then the harder you pulled to get them off, the tighter they became.

Even if her parents would have succeeded in getting the young girl to swallow a morsel of food, all she had to do to "win" this epic battle was throw up. The child had clearly claimed her power to decide if she was going to live or die. That's why the therapist's first order of healing business was to redistribute the power in this family. She had too much power, and the parents didn't have enough. Respect for personal boundaries in this family was all but gone, and so was any sense of personal responsibility.

It was clear to my fellow students and me that the parents needed to put their energy toward something they *could* change. The answer to that would be for both parents to turn the focus upon themselves. That way they could each regain not only their personal power but also a sense of direction and purpose. That kind of self-generated power can't be taken by another. That is the power of self-love. That is what "Try Softer" is ultimately all about.

From a clinical perspective, I recognized that the first thing both parents needed to do was surrender to the truth. The therapist knew that meant the father needed to go through this humiliating and frightening drama, just to exhaust all options. Both parents had to finally admit that, even if it meant their daughter's death, they could not make her eat.

Once the parents accepted that trying harder was doomed to fail, they agreed to take a softer path. That's when a considerable amount of pressure was relieved from the girl. With the therapist's help, the parents learned that by taking the spotlight off of their daughter and shining the light of truth upon themselves and their own issues, everyone could begin to heal.

The following explanation is an over-simplified Family-Therapy perspective

Generally speaking, because the parents had issues between themselves that they either didn't want to address or weren't ready or able to take an honest look at, they had triangulated their problems onto their daughter. In that way, they (subconsciously) *used* their daughter as a distraction from their own personal and relationship issues. It's as if their daughter's desperate message was: *"Hey, Mom and Dad. Look at me. Look here. Keep your focus on me. That way you won't need to face the painful issues between the two of you.*

I'm afraid if you acknowledge your relationship issues, you will separate and abandon me."

In this case—and I've seen it work this way in many other families as well—the girl was, at some level of consciousness, willing to help her parents avoid the pain of facing the issues between them. Regarding role assignment within the family system, she was willing to be their protector, even at the risk of her own life. Such "sacrificial lambs" in a family are often the ones who take on the role of the deflector. They become the sick one, or the bad one, even to their own detriment. The family system keeps operating but in a dysfunctional and destructive way. It's like a bump in a tire. Even when the bump becomes dangerously distracting, and a warning, the wheel keeps going round and round. In family-therapy terms, individuals—and it is not always a child—who take most of the heat are called the *white sheep* of the family. They are usually the strongest individuals in the family system. As counter-intuitive as it seems, this frail little girl, wasting away to nothing, was actually the most courageous family member. And in many ways, the strongest.

The child's (subconscious) motivation for getting sick in the first place was to keep her parents together. In the process, as unhealthy and painful as it was, she gained the "reward" of having their attention, 24 hours a day. While most children would, at some level, appreciate such parental interest and attention, in this case, the constant focus on their daughter was hurting everyone—making the *whole* family sick.

We all know that healthy family togetherness is a wonderful thing. Parents and children who look after each other—work, play, live and love together—are the happiest people around. This is true as long as things don't get too out of balance.

When a family member, parent or child—by choice or imposition—becomes an enabler, shield or scapegoat by absolving themselves of self-responsibility, they are bound to pay a heavy price. To the extent any family member places responsibility for their own health and happiness on another, the system, generally, will only spiral down.

Perhaps ironically, in the case at hand, the young girl finally accomplished her original goal of helping her parents stay together. The car got a whole new tire. Once her parents lifted their extreme focus off of her and accepted the healthy restructuring of the family system offered by the therapist, the frail teen relaxed into the most natural thing for any human to do — eating.

You're not saying the parents should have just ignored their daughter's problem in the first place, are you? No. And thank God they didn't. No, I'm just pointing out that their daughter's problem was connected to and in some ways a symptom of her parents' undercurrent of unresolved issues. It was the therapist's mission to discover, uncover and heal whatever issues were preventing each family member from relaxing into their own personal alignment. In this case, I am happy to say it worked out beautifully. I know, because I had the privilege of watching several successive sessions with this family.

Note to concerned parents.

It's not true, in every case where children act out or develop a chronic problem or disease, that the parents are the cause or even part of the problem. And they are rarely solely to blame. But the same may be said of the children. As I mentioned above, placing blame serves no purpose. When it comes to "owning" any problem, however, it often helps to think in terms of relationship dynamics. Generally speaking, each individual plays some kind of purposeful part in their family system. This includes the children. And consciously or unconsciously, just because we are human, everyone tends to adopt a "role" or behavior pattern particularly suitable to them. Such patterns can help to heal family issues, or they can contribute to maintaining dysfunction.

If you know of a child suffering from any kind of eating disorder, I suggest that you look into the family-therapy path of treatment, along with considering all other options. I've seen so many cases of Anorexia and other related types of illnesses and issues effectively cured, using the Family-Therapy mode of treatment, that I must, in all good conscience, at least recommend it as a possible option.

It always helps to keep psychology's most fundamental tenant in mind. Which is:

All behavior is purposeful.

Once you realize that people *always* have reasons for what they do, even when you can't imagine what those reasons could be, you become more understanding. When you become more understanding, your heart naturally opens. That's when blocks and barriers start to fall away. You begin feeling more empathetic toward others. And you automatically become more tolerant and less judgmental. With enough growth, you get to the point where you can't imagine trying to *force* anyone to do anything.

The more you criticize, judge or condemn others, the more incentive you give them to continue behaving exactly how you don't want them to. If you don't believe me, try badgering someone into quitting smoking or giving up any bad habit.

Discover and use softer, more effective, ways to help your loved ones.

For example, and always with the greatest respect:

• Offer to be there for them to assist them in making any changes they would like to, if and when they decide they need help.

- Let them know that you fully understand their right to make their own decisions. Assure them that your concerns are out of love and only about the consequences of their actions.
- Strengthen your overall relationship with the person you are trying to help by supporting them every way you can. Make your goal not to change them, but rather to change yourself to be a better friend.
- The most important thing you can do to influence the behavior of another is to model the behavior you think would serve them better. If you are 50 pounds overweight, for example, you might not be in the best position to advise others to eat more vegetables. It's difficult for many to accept the truth that you really cannot control another, no matter how hard you try. The "Try Softer" way is to inspire them to want to make changes for themselves. The most powerful way to do that is to set a good example by taking care of yourself.

Chapter 3

Being Your Own Soulmate

"Trying Softer" means appreciating, honoring and loving your Self.

The Three Most Valuable Keys to Self-Acceptance I've learned along my journey are:

1) Have loving allowance for all things to be in their own time and place, beginning with yourself.

2) With respect, increase your communication with all of life.

3) Embrace self-responsibility, understanding that it is through your choices and perceptions that you are continuously creating your own reality.

A common misguided notion that many people have embedded in their thought process is that it's a selfish thing to take care of yourself. This is because so many of us have been taught that the most righteous and noble thing, even if not the healthiest thing, is to sacrifice our own needs for the needs of our loved ones.

It's certainly a rewarding thing to help others, anyway and anytime we can. I believe that is why we are born in the first place. It's certainly why I'm writing this book. When the need is there, such as with parents and their children or when children become adults and take care of their aging parents, we want and need to make every sacrifice we can to care for our family. That's just being loving. Not only is it a loving thing to do, but it is also soul-nurturing for the caregiver as well. The issue, of course, becomes one of balance.

If we go too far in the direction of denying our own needs, in favor of the needs of another, such as sacrificing basic things like eating and sleeping for extended periods, we will start to feel resentment toward the one we are caring for. When self-sacrifice becomes martyrdom, everybody suffers. Studies in nursing homes show that over-extended caregivers tend to treat their patients less kindly and less conscientiously than rested and balanced workers. You need to take care of yourself to give others what they need and deserve.

Most likely, since you are reading this book, you have probably already given yourself permission to feel happier and healthier on your path. But it is surprising how many people don't believe they deserve to feel better. If you have any guilt about working on yourself, following your dreams, and living your most authentic life on your own terms, it may help to think about it this way: **You can share only what you have**. Right? Conversely, of course, you can't share what you don't have.

Consider what that means regarding your personality and your overall state of health. For example, if you are run down, depressed, sick and tired of being sick and tired, then (because that's all you have) that is what you will share with others. They may want, need or wish for you to be more uplifting, helpful and inspiring, but if all you have is misery, that's all they'll get from you. If you are miserable and preoccupied with your own struggles, you cannot be available for them.

On the other hand, if you are feeling even reasonably healthy and balanced, then you will have something supportive, positive and healthy to offer your loved ones. Whether that's your time and attention, your affection, your wisdom, your caring heart, or nothing more than a laugh, you can help your friend. And every time we help another, we help ourselves.

Taking care of yourself is the most *generous and loving* thing you can do for everyone. Your loved ones deserve to have the best version of you that you can allow to manifest. That's a win-win for everyone.

Loving allowance means accepting how things are within yourself and in the outside world. Things are how they are. That's simply the truth.

If you want to change anything or anybody, you'll need to begin by changing yourself. For example, if you'd like your partner to be kinder or more understanding, your best bet is to stop working on him or her and begin aligning yourself more with your own heart. That is something you can change. If you want the sun to come out when it is raining, that is something you cannot change. Your best bet in that situation is to pray for a rainbow. In both cases, in fact in all cases, no matter how you want your world to be different, you can change only yourself. "Allowing for" doesn't necessarily mean condoning. It just means accepting that whatever it is, is the case right now.

Of course, because everything is always changing, what is the case right now will not be the case even a moment from now. The best way for you to act and react in the ever-evolving fabric of the universe — of which you are a part but do not fully control — is to keep relaxing into a more centered place of acceptance. In other words, fight less against yourself and all that is. The more relaxed you are, the more centered and balanced, and the less afraid and frustrated, the more effective your actions will be. That translates to increased health and happiness in your life.

Increased Communication means letting the world know who you are and how you feel, always with respect. It means speaking up for yourself and sharing your authenticity. *Communication* in the broadest sense also includes communing with nature. It means feeling alive. It means not keeping life at arm's length. It means what Wayne Dyer once wrote to me:

"Tom, Thanks for a beautiful letter. Indeed, we are exchanging gifts. By all means, write your book and don't die with your music still in you. I send you all my love and a 'green' light. Wayne."

The *with respect* part of the equation is huge. We really need to get back to respecting one another. What happened to the Golden Rule? If only we could just stop for a second, as we go about our daily business with the world, and ask ourselves "How would I like to be treated in this situation?" Wow, there would be so much less conflict. So much less blame and anger. And so much more empathy, sharing, caring, harmony and love! It comes back to that great question we should continually be asking ourselves:
"Hmmm…Would I rather be right or kind?"

*Here's a great key to improve not only your communication skills but everything about your life. Plus it's a dandy lead-in to the next part about self-responsibility:

If you remember nothing else from this book, the following phrase will change your life. You'll be doing yourself the greatest favor each time you make the choice to **respond, rather than react.**

Instead of having a Pavlovian-like response of instantly reacting to what others say and do, and then blaming them for making you feel and act a certain way, try taking a few seconds to pause, breathe… and then *decide how best to respond.*

Responding is so much healthier and productive than turning over your personal power to others and reacting like a victim of whatever buttons they want to push. The key is to realize that how you think, act, and — even feel — is a choice. Even if a thousand people gather around you and call you a jerk, that reveals nothing about you and everything about the thousand jerks present. You are not what anyone says you are. You are what and how you decide to be. The key is to release fear-based, ego-protecting mental blocks, replace negative self-talk with more kind and loving thoughts about yourself, and allow yourself to blossom into the uniquely authentic person you were born to be. It really doesn't matter what others think when it comes to being the captain of your own destiny.

Being a conscious communicator and taking full responsibility for your thoughts, feelings, and actions enables you to have a fuller, happier, less stressful life. But that can't happen as long as you think others are making you be the way you are.

Self-Responsibility means owning who you are. It means accepting responsibility for all that you say and do and accepting responsibility for the consequences. It means standing in your truth. Standing in your truth does not mean insisting that you are right. It simply means you have the right to be yourself. The opposite of self-responsibility, of course, is blaming others for one's own behavior. Aside from causing problems because of the passing of the buck to another, not accepting self-responsibility puts you in a no-win bind. For one thing, if you don't accept ownership for what you've contributed, behaviorwise, then if things work out you can't take the credit. And I have yet to meet someone who couldn't use another well-deserved pat on the back.

The other big problem is because with freedom comes responsibility; to the extent you don't take responsibility for your decisions and actions, you limit your freedom to grow and live a healthy life.

What I like most about these three healthy, helpful growth tools or tenets is how they work so beautifully in tandem. Once you get used to them and apply them, you'll see how they flow together naturally.

What happens is: When you employ one round of loving allowance, increased communication, and self-responsibility... it begets another. The next round then becomes a deeper and more unified version of the same kind of openness, but with more profound growth and self-understanding. This continuing process of self-acceptance, increased communication and self-responsibility then becomes a never-ending journey of self-discovery and awareness.

Applying these three principles in tandem, in your daily life, results in a heart-opening spiral of continuous mind/body/spirit growth and expansion. Allowing your consciousness to dance with these combined principles enables you to grow into ever better versions of yourself. Such a process—such a heart-path-leads to wholeness, happiness, and fulfillment. It is a beautiful and natural way to relax into spiritual alignment.

In terms of gaining self-knowledge and awareness, asking yourself the following kinds of introspective questions can be helpful:

1) Am I doing all the things I can to become the best version of myself?

2) Am I as kind as I can be? Am I as patient and understanding as I am capable of?

3) Am I making a difference in the lives of others?

4) When someone is talking to me, do I truly listen? Am I fighting to be right, rather than kind?

5) Am I keeping my heart open and trying soft enough to keep my ego in balance?

6) Am I afraid to face certain fears?

7) Am I willing to forgive myself and others for wrong-doing and injustice?

8) Do I care about the difference my life makes to others?

9) Do I realize how precious and tentative life really is?

10) Do I realize that not risking is a risk in itself?

Acknowledging that, inside of your being you know who and how you are, is practicing **Loving Allowance**, beginning with yourself.

Asking your internal being to provide information about who and how you are, to your conscious mind, is practicing **Increased Communication** with life (of which you are a part) with respect.

Accepting the honest answer to any such questions is applying greater and more loving allowance. And when you make a change in your way of behaving, based on honest information from within, you are practicing **Self-Responsibility.**

Trying softer is not complicated. It is the simplest, most natural way to be. All you have to do is relax into your most authentic self. Think of it like sinking into a hammock. Once you begin to accept that this level of honesty is the healthiest way to think, grow and be, and how much better off you are for not blocking it, then you really start to experience a Life Worth Living. It's all about getting to accept, know and love yourself, first, so that you can get to accept, know, and love others as well. How is that not the best way to honor God?

Love Yourself

A Reading Meditation

Appreciate Your Physical Self

Have loving allowance for everything about your physical body including its color, shape, gender, age, state of health and size. Rather than judging or attacking it, appreciate your body for the divine vessel it is. It's the only body you have. Why not get to know it, love it and have a healthy relationship with it?

Instead of comparing your body with anyone else's, allow yourself to appreciate your beautiful uniqueness. Just like your fingerprints, your laugh, and the way you walk, everything about your body is a one-of-a-kind representation in the Universe. That's an incredibly miraculous thing!

Increase communication with your body, with respect. Let your body know that you are honored to take care of it. Allow all barriers between you and your body to melt away. Release any anger you might feel toward your body. Listen to what it is telling you. Take a loving interest in your body by sensing, hearing, feeling, noticing and caring what's going on with it, more consciously every day. For example:

What is your stomach saying to you right now? Your chest? Your throat? Can you feel your heart? What parts of your body are asking for attention? What parts of your body are saying, "I'm just fine"? Let your body know how much you appreciate how it is keeping you safe as you experience life. Touch your body. Show it affection. Be proud of the body God gave you. Allow all resistance between you and your body to fade away.

Honor your body as the divine temple it is by adopting a healthy way of eating and giving it all the water it needs. Be forever grateful to and for your body. Where would you be without it? Check into the benefits of a plant-based diet. It may change your life!

Appreciate Your Intellectual Self

Talk to your intellectual self. Communicate with great respect to the thinking part of you. Have loving allowance for your internal dialogue to be whatever it is. When you think it may be helpful, include self-reflection and analysis.

Appreciate your intuition as well as your common sense. Appreciate also the abilities to discover, discern, dissect and discriminate that your intellect contributes to your life. Be grateful for your infinitely vast imagination. Thank it for being such a wellspring of creativity.

Praise your intellect for its amazing problem-solving capabilities. Send gratitude, appreciation, and love to all parts of yourself that help you organize your world. Love how your brain allows you to do everything, including how to analyze sensory input, draw conclusions, make decisions, have opinions, and accumulate knowledge. Honor your intellect with thoughts of deep appreciation.

Listen to your self-chatter. What are you saying to yourself right now? Is the "real you" the innocent bystander of this ongoing conversation, or the creator? Once you realize that you can change your internal dialogue and make it more loving, forgiving and less judgmental, you will feel much better about yourself. Accepting self-responsibility at such a deep level is life changing.

Is your heart part of your intellectual self? Does it have a mind of its own? Does it send messages to you? Is there a back and forth between your heart and your mind? Is there harmony there? Would you like to enjoy more feelings of peace, harmony, and love within yourself, as you experience every kind of thought and feeling? Allow your Self to help you with those beautiful desires. Every resource is within.

Appreciate Your Spiritual Self

Your Spirituality is your connection with all things. It is where you come from, where you reside, and where you are going. It is the essence of you. It is what you are sensing when you are aware that there must be more to you than just a body — more to you than even your body, thoughts, and feelings. Are you not part of the same nature that produces all of life? Don't all human beings breathe the same air and look with wonder at the same sky? Do you think you are one drop in the vast ocean? Or do you realize you are the vast ocean in one drop?

Lovingly allow that your Spirituality is you, as you experience life, learning and growing from your experiences. It's not some mystical segment or part of yourself buried away. As you work, play and love—indeed, each time you take a breath—you do so as a spiritual being having human experiences. Allow yourself to embrace any point of view that feels right to you, regarding religion and spirituality. Trust, if it opens your heart and serves to bring you peace, that your faith is based upon your unique recognition of a deep truth offered from your spiritual self. Respect the rights of others to find their own way back to their heart, love, and God.

Your ultimate perspective on any subject is a spiritual one, considering everything you do is by, for, because of, or on behalf of your Spirit or Soul. Your Spirit, your Soul, your highest or deepest self is Of the Source. You have within you the energy, not only of life but of eternal life. That energy is God's Love. You are an eternal being, an aspect of God, connected to the Universe—a part of everything. As a member of the human family, you are in equal standing with everyone in the eyes of God. You are akin to nature and connected to—indeed, made up of—all of life's natural elements. No matter who you are, or what you believe about yourself, or what you've done or failed to do, The Universe, Nature, God, Life, Love (whatever you choose to call the Divine Source) is on your side and in your heart.

You can never be disconnected from God. Where else could authentic power, consciousness, love, and life force energy come from? You are a spiritual being having a human experience, not the other way around. In all kinds of miraculous ways, your body is like a glove with God's hand inside.

Feeling the Power

The times when we are most ourselves are the times when we are lost in activities we enjoy. In such moments we are plugged into the power of being alive in the present moment, not trapped in our egos. Some call those times of being in the zone. I call such moments "Dancing with your Higher Self."

You are dancing with your Higher Self each time:
- You are having fun
- You are lost in thought
- You are playing a sport, and you enter "the Zone"
- You are speaking from your heart
- You are creating something from your imagination
- You are totally engrossed in study, work or play
- You are listening to or playing music
- You are surprised
- You are laughing
- You are sleeping or half-awake
- You are making love
- You are petting an animal
- You are comforting a loved one
- You are smelling a flower
- You are playing with a child
- You are enjoying fond memories
- You are engrossed in a good book
- You are singing
- You are praying
- You are caught up in wonder
- You are crying
- You are enjoying nature
- You are hugging someone
- You are dancing
- You are meditating

The above experiences come from "Trying Softer." You can't enjoy them if you are too discontented, blocked, frustrated or otherwise bent on trying harder. If you try to force fun, it's not fun anymore.

The Most Powerful Person in the World

The most powerful person on the planet isn't the general of the biggest army. Nor is it the greatest weightlifter in the world, or the wealthiest person. It's not even the president. The most powerful person in the world is a baby.

Politicians can have great influence, of course, but they can also, at least in theory, be voted out. They have only as much power as the people give them. Babies are born with almost infinite power. In terms of our "Try Softer" thesis, babies are the best examples of how to change the world with no effort.

Think about the power an infant has. As soon as it's born, every family member's life is instantly and forever changed. Especially the mother's. What won't we do to care for a baby? Aside from diapers, we gladly change our work situations, our home environments, our school districts, take extra jobs to start saving for education, and do our best to learn greater patience and how to become a better nurturer, teacher and provider. From the moment the baby is born, its parents make the necessary adjustments in their own lives to care for the new little emperor.

While I set that up in kind of cute terms, it really is true. Vulnerability is the ultimate strength. That's not saying that weakness is strength. Weakness is weakness. Genuine vulnerability and helplessness inspire humans to step up and help one another. It evokes the desire to care for and protect those among us who cannot fend for themselves. It evokes the power of compassion. The most natural thing in the world is for parents, even in the animal kingdom, to care for their young. Such is the power of love—a power all of us have access to all the time.

For many of us, to ask for help is difficult. It is often a last resort because we are afraid to be perceived as weak. In truth, because it requires vulnerability, it is the strongest statement we can make. The wounded and dying, such as on the battlefield, commonly call out for their mothers. That's because they have nothing to lose. At that moment, they could not be more real. They are not hung up on ego or image, or fear of what another person might think of them. Their cries are the most real utterances a human can make. Their pleas are the last remnants of any strength they may have left.

So here we have another clue about "Trying Softer." **"Trying Softer" means letting go of ego and concerns about image or what others might think. Trying softer means relaxing into accepting the power you were granted at birth: the power to be totally honest, authentic, open, and in touch with your spirituality as well as your physicality. Most importantly, it means embracing your need, willingness and "strength" to ask for and accept help from others.**

You might think you are making this life trip alone. You're not. You need help from everybody. We all need as much help as we can get from everyone. That's how strong we all are.

Recently, I was the guest therapist at a meeting for abused women. The group's name, as well as its goal, is: Overcoming Powerlessness. As the participants were all mothers, I brought up the baby analogy, and it made them smile. I asked them: "If your goal is to become more powerful, where do you think the power supply wellspring is, that you can draw from to recharge? In other words," I said, answering my own question, "who has your power if it's not already within you?"

Through discussion about what power is and isn't, and distinguishing between power and force, most of the participants began to recognize that the power supply is within themselves. It is in their hearts, their souls and their trust in God, Life, the Universe and Love — all of those things a baby depends on to survive.

The only real power in the Universe is LOVE. When you have love in your heart and a desire to live a life most "right" for you—in full accordance with your unique mission on earth—then you are POWERFUL! You are powerful because you are not blocking all of life's divine energy. Babies never block anything, and the whole wide world pretty much accommodates them all along the way. Except when horrendous things happen because weak people—not powerful people or strong people—use force to abuse them.

But we grownups are no longer helpless infants. So we can use our developed brains and senses to take self-responsible steps to advocate for ourselves, defend ourselves, take care of ourselves, honor ourselves, respect ourselves, and, most importantly, ask everyone around us to help us. We never outgrow that need.

If you want to feel less like a victim, you need to realize two things:

One) That you deserve happiness and to always be treated with respect.

Two) That you are the only one you can change.

You can't force anyone (even yourself) to change. When it comes to changing things about yourself, often the biggest challenge is to allow a better version of yourself to emerge. The best version of who you are, and were meant to be, is always within you. That pristine, clean-slated infant, with full potential to be a perfectly suited, kind, happy and healthy contributing member of the human family, is still rooted in your soul. That loving spirit—that wellspring of infinite possibilities—is who you most truly and essentially are. It's the place, the person, the feeling, the way and the health you need to get back to. All you need to do is set your intention, based on full alignment—mind/body and spirit—let go of all of the fear-based blocks you can feel inside, and then allow the Universe to renew and restore you to yourself. That's what "Try Softer" means.

You are a miracle — a perfect, multidimensional child of God, a Priceless Treasure and Shining Star. You are nothing less than a Lighthouse of Love — a Beacon of Hope guiding the rest of us back into the safe harbor of our own Hearts.

"Hold her steady, hon. I'm gonna drive this baby home in one swing!"

Chapter 4

You are Your Own Opponent

"Trying Softer" is for everyone, even "real" men.

"Trying Softer" is an equal opportunity life strategy. It can benefit anyone, anytime. This includes "real" men. Soft does not mean *weak*. On the contrary. "Trying Softer" allows more power to surface, generally enabling a *stronger* result. This is because if you are relaxed and unblocked enough, to begin with, then, if and when force is necessary, it will be able to explode forth in a less restricted, more efficient way.

For example, police officers suddenly faced with a life-or-death situation may not have time to ponder their reactions. Instead, they must rely upon their reflexes, instincts and natural flight or fight responses. If well-trained, instead of freezing up and blocking themselves with fear, insecurity or self-doubt, they will be able to react appropriately.

Force driven by anger, frustration or fear will not be as effective as force powered by loving intentions. Examples of *superhuman* strength are found in those cases we sometimes hear about; such as the 130-pound mother at the scene of an accident who, through the power of love, was able to lift the back of the car to free her child's leg from under the wheel. Yes, that's adrenaline. But it's more than that. Such superhuman events are examples of the kind of faith that can "move mountains."

The strongest muscle you have is your brain. Or maybe it's your heart, as is the case when little people lift big cars. Ultimately, it's your will to accomplish what you want to achieve. People who rely on their bodies to make a living, such as athletes, know the importance of being psychologically, emotionally and physically balanced. Let's consider boxers.

Float like a butterfly, sting like a bee.

To Ringside! Imagine you are seated in a big, smelly boxing arena in Kinshasa, Zaire. The year is 1974. You have a front row seat for the *fight of the century* — billed as "The Rumble in the Jungle!" And here you are!

(I'm sure you're wondering how you got here. Only a few seconds ago, you were sitting in a comfortable chair reading this book!)

George Foreman enters the ring! He looks fierce and determined. He's full of energy and obviously ready to defend his title. His unlikely challenger, Muhammad Ali, climbs into the ring also. He seems less fired up.

DING! The bell sounds to start the first round! The big men touch gloves. You're already rooting for the underdog. Because of Foreman's powerful record, however, you're secretly expecting Foreman to drop Ali within a few rounds.

As the two combatants dance around the ring, things liven up quickly. Each man tries to dominate the other. They start swinging. Bam! Umph! Boom-Boom-Boom! Dodging and weaving all over the place, man! The fight is on! Both boxers are hungry to draw blood. The crowd is electrified! You're on the edge of your seat! In fact, you're yelling and cursing like everybody else. (*I know that's not like you, but given the environment, you're hardly aware of what you're saying!*) You feel strangely self-conscious not having a cigar in your teeth. It's just all part of the atmosphere. The fighter's loud grunts are shocking. "Umph-Umph!" Sweat is spraying everywhere. Wow, you think to yourself, this is a real fight! These guys are trying to kill each other! No wonder! Think of all the money and prestige at stake!

By the middle of the second round, you begin to realize that only one boxer is trying to kill the other. That would be wild man Foreman! He's like a crazed pit bull. He just keeps pounding Ali with jackhammer-like punches: Boom-Boom-Boom-Boom-Boom!

But Ali, the challenger, seems strangely composed. He's even spending a lot of time leaning on the ropes. Yet he keeps taunting Foreman to punch him harder! What's going on here? Ali can't be running out of gas already? Can he? You're thinking to yourself: Man, if Ali doesn't get more into the fight, his face will be flat on the mat soon!

But what neither you nor George Foreman is aware of is that Muhammad Ali knows exactly what he is doing. He is purposely baiting Foreman into *trying too hard*. The challenger is using his (now) famous *Rope-a-Dope* technique (akin to what I'm calling a "Try Softer" — more relaxed — approach). Using such a smart strategy, Ali is conserving energy by "resting" against the ropes.

For at least six of the first seven rounds, Foreman keeps charging straight into Ali's trap. In doing so, he gradually depletes his energy trying to knock out his *smart-ass* challenger.

When the opening bell for round eight sounds, Ali pounces from his corner, freshly invigorated with reserve energy. Within seconds he pounds the exhausted Foreman to the mat.

The referee stops the fight! Muhammad Ali is pronounced the new Heavyweight Champion of the World!

One of many things that made Muhammad Ali a world champion boxer was his high degree of self-knowledge. The Champ knew that no matter whom he faced in the ring, his most formidable opponent was always himself. He understood that in all aspects of life, the key is always to relax, pace yourself and not try too hard. Of course, in the ring, Ali also understood the psychology of each boxer he faced. He was a natural student of human nature. His book, "Soul of a Butterfly," contains many valuable life lessons about following your dreams.

Muhammad Ali grew to become a renowned teacher and advocate for human rights, understanding that the gaining of respect can never be forced. It must be earned — the soft way.

Bruce Lee advised his students:

"Be like water making its way through cracks. Do not be assertive, but adjust to the object, and you shall find a way around or through it. If nothing within you stays rigid, outward things will disclose themselves. Empty your mind, be formless. Shapeless, like water."

To be Your Authentic Self means

* To be rooted in and committed to your own truth, as you recognize it within, rather than being subject to or swayed by the opinions of others.

* To know who you are, given your particular strengths and weaknesses, likes and dislikes, preferences, attitude, and aptitudes, and to respect, honor and share those and every other aspect of you with others — with all due love and respect toward them.

* To be accepting and aware of your feelings, as well as your thoughts and perceptions, and then to make the most

responsible choices you can, based on an honest and complete self-understanding.

* To not be afraid to own and acknowledge your total self, and to walk your deepest, truest, most important walk.

* To be confident enough to say "no" when that is in your own best interest, and to walk away from situations in which you can't be yourself.

To *not* be your authentic self or to pretend you are some other kind of person, whether in a given situation or as a way of living your life, requires you to block yourself from your natural spiritual alignment.

The only way I was able to help Helen, the lady in the story that opened Chapter One, was to make sure my heart was unrestricted when I was with her. To do that, I had to completely surrender to God, the Universe, Love and Life. I had to get myself out of my own way. Intuitively, I knew that Helen needed more than a clever psychologist's ideas, techniques or therapeutic strategies. So I laid my bag of tools aside, and I released all fear. Her extreme vulnerability inspired me to risk being completely vulnerable myself. Helen's obvious and excruciating pain and suffering melted away any part of my ego that might have blocked my need to give — and her need to receive — unconditional love.

The real me, my essence, my most authentic self — just like for you and everyone else — is Love. Love is the energy that flows through all living things, once fear-based blocks are removed. Sometimes, to try harder, (rather than softer) to do something, we end up creating more blocks to the healing power of the Universe. Your life will become a lot less stressful once you realize the benefits of not allowing your ego to block the expression, and expansion, of your most authentic self. All you need to do is allow yourself to feel vulnerable. Which only means — to be open.

The Strength of Vulnerability

Many of us have grown up being taught that revealing our true feelings is somehow a sign of weakness. This is especially true for boys. The unfortunate and misguided sentiment in the minds of too many people is that it is ok, even expected, for girls to cry because they are the "weaker sex" anyway, but not so for boys. I guess if you are making a comparison based on the assumption that "strength" is *solely* defined by testosterone levels and weightlifting ability, then yes, you might be able to identify a "weaker" gender. Of course, such a narrow focus would reflect little understanding of what true strength is and means for human beings. Once you understand that non-physical strength is all about honesty, openness, courage, fortitude, will, trust, authenticity, and vulnerability, then you realize it is an admirable trait found equally in men and women. That's because real strength comes from love. And love is the essence of all human beings. Weak is how one feels when such true and loving energy is denied, deflected, disavowed, ignored or otherwise blocked.

Naturally, all human beings are capable of demonstrating both weakness and strength in varying ways and degrees under any and all circumstances. Concerning our "Try Softer" understanding, the more unblocked you are, the stronger you are. When you are unblocked, spiritually aligned, and caught in the act of being your truest self, then it may be said that you are as strong as you can be in your own personhood. Again, *strong* ultimately means honest, real and authentic, and open to the natural flow of life.

In reality, we are all vulnerable all the time. Being subject to and open to all kinds of experiences, happenings, events, and circumstances — none of which we can have complete control over, all the time — is the basic definition of what it means to be alive. Though we like to think we can put up armor and build impenetrable defenses and hide, even from ourselves, we really cannot be completely protected from anything. We can't protect ourselves from life because we *are* life.

You are life in the form of a Living You. If you were no longer vulnerable to feeling certain things, you would not be able to experience the fullness of life. To experience the highs, we have to be open to experiencing the lows. We need to be open to experiencing pain, in order to experience joy. Trying not to be vulnerable is the same thing as trying not to be alive.

Of course, nobody likes pain. But it is inevitably part of the human experience. Often, we create problems for ourselves — including bringing more pain into our lives — when we block the flow of all of life in an effort to avoid facing uncomfortable parts of ourselves.

Many of us try to deny that we are vulnerable (to being hurt) by either ignoring our true feelings or trying to numb them. Ultimately, in either case, you can't fool Mother Nature. Repressed feelings always find some way and some place within you to manifest. Over time, stored-up emotions and pent-up feelings start to manifest their energy in the form of dis-ease.

We also know that numbing our feelings doesn't help anybody either. Especially those persons who think that hiding their head or heart in the sand is to their benefit. Addictions such as working all the time, drinking to excess, exercising to extreme, sleeping to avoid facing issues and other forms of avoidance behavior never work in the long run. They only delay the inevitable, which is facing yourself.

The reason I call this chapter "You are Your Own Opponent" is because you are. Just as you are your own soulmate, best friend and greatest partner. Whatever you want to do or hope to accomplish hour-to-hour, day-to-day or in the course of your lifetime, you will have to do it in full accordance with all parts of yourself. This is the old, sort of, joke — but not really — that "Me, Myself and I" need to learn how to get along.

The "Try Softer" way is to not get into battles with yourself.

The "Try Softer" way is to accept who and how you are.

The "Try Softer" way is to allow yourself to feel everything that you feel.

The "Try Softer" way is to allow the love of the Universe to flow through you and to guide and assist you in all endeavors.

Three myths about vulnerability

Vulnerability is weakness.

As we've already discussed, being open, aware and honest is not weakness. Admitting and accepting that it is scary to feel exposed in any way is a great sign of psychological health in and of itself. Ultimately, if there is such a thing as "security" in this world (and being safe from anything) the "truth" is the only possible sanctuary. That's because nothing can get under or behind the truth. It stands firm as a representation of itself. It can be assaulted, insulted and attacked from every angle, yet the truth remains intact. The truth doesn't have to be recognized, understood or even acknowledged, yet it stands. So if you want to protect yourself from unwanted feelings—such as embarrassment or shame—your best bet is to admit it and get it out there first. Face it. Then it can't be brought down. A tree grounded in the truth can never be uprooted. Not admitting you are vulnerable is weakness. That is denying your humanness. In the end, no one can get away with that without painful consequences.

Vulnerability means revealing your most embarrassing secrets.

Just because you are admitting that you are vulnerable, and even willing to reveal your real self, does not mean you have to go up to the mail carrier and spill your guts. You never have to relinquish your right to be discerning and discriminating regarding who has the right to know what about you. Opening yourself up, by choice, as risky as that may seem, is actually the best way to maintain self-control. To the extent you try to fool your body by acting like you don't feel however you do, you will be headed for a loss of control. You know how it goes when you try to hold in your anger after an argument with a spouse or partner—eventually, whether gradually or in one big explosion, it comes out. Better to accept it and admit it in the first place.

Of course, we are talking about communication here. Communication, first, between you and yourself (you deciding what parts of yourself you want to hide, deny, try to protect, or reveal) and then between you and others. In most, if not all, cases, honesty truly is the best policy. All you need to do is accept that you are not a superhero or a robot. Rather, accept, embrace and celebrate the fact that you are a multidimensional, spiritual being having a human experience.

The greatest show of strength is self-acceptance. That's because self-acceptance is Life-acceptance. And Life acceptance is God-acceptance. Denying "what is" always has negative consequences. Sometimes the greatest risk is in not risking at all. Besides, most of the time when we think we are fooling ourselves or another person by "acting" a certain way, they "know" the real scoop anyway. How many times have you withheld something like a "secret" from a loved one only to find out after you confess that they "knew it all along." Just be honest. There is nothing shameful about being human.

Vulnerability reflects poor character.

A strong, honest, heart-connected person is not a person of poor or deficient character. Once you understand that vulnerability is simply honesty and openness, it's difficult to defame a person for being so real. Such a judgment would reflect more upon the accuser than upon the one being attacked for not wearing more psychological armor.

The key is to come from your heart. Your heart, though subject to being hurt—and sometimes feeling like it is even broken—is the strongest part of your being. It's the most trustworthy, most true, and real thing about you. Your ego and your self-chatter can fool you and lead you off track. But your heart will give you only truth. Always trust your heart.

It takes real strength to say and mean such things as:

* "No, thank you."

* "I'm sorry."

* "Can you help me?"

* "I don't understand."

* "I was wrong."

* "It was my fault."

* "I apologize."

* "Will you forgive me?"

* "I'm afraid."

* "I'm embarrassed."

* "I'm feeling angry." (or any other feeling)

* "I don't know what to say."

* "I love you."

*And so many other things that are scary, but oh so healing and healthy to reveal.

"Soft is stronger than hard, water stronger than rocks, love stronger than force." **Hermann Hesse**

Using Soft Power *means*

*Allowing your best and strongest qualities to work for you, rather than sabotaging yourself because of too much fear, anger, impatience, aggression or frustration.

*Caring enough to take time to do the job right, rather than messing it up at first and then having to do it over.

*Being passionate enough and determined enough not to allow anything to keep you from doing your very best.

*Staying focused and committed, no matter what challenges emerge, to remain open, adaptable and going with the flow. It means keeping the faith—steady as she goes.

*Whether you are a man or woman, young or old, rich or poor, healthy or not, if you have a task to do, any task, your chances of successfully completing that task are greater if you mentally relax, concentrate, accept help from other sources, and hold your focus, rather than recklessly or too impulsively or aggressively charging forward.

*Being open to every kind of help and support. Most importantly, power from your own natural inner resources: all energies connected with God, Love, Spirit, and Life.

*Accepting that pain is a part of life. Nobody grows without pain. We suffer when we accumulate blocks to our happiness, and it sometimes hurts as much to remove them.

Affirmation of Self

I am a child of God, a once-in-the-Universe creation.

There will never be another person just like me.

I have my own fingerprints, walk and laugh.

My decisions are mine, as are the consequences they create.

I own all of my feelings, reflections, and flutters of my heart.

I own all of me — my body, mind, and spirit. And I love all of me.

I own my ideas, dreams, hopes, feelings, and fantasies, whether joyful or painful.

I reserve the right to think, feel and behave differently from others as I grant them the same freedoms.

I own my failures, missteps, and mistakes as well as my triumphs and successes, and whether I learn from the consequences I create.

When it comes to forgiveness, I look first in my own heart.

I laugh freely and loudly at myself, have fun being who and how I am, and do not judge, criticize or try to change others.

I have a reverence for all of Life.

We don't have to be so insensitive, robotic, predictable, conforming and non-flexible in our communications. It's a matter of choice. In order to meet our fundamental need for intimacy, we must learn how to present ourselves as real human beings, rather than acting like stoic, hardened characters and caricatures of who we think others want to see. The key is to loosen up — relax — and "Try Softer." Staying rigid and holding firm to a way of being that you think serves you better than realness, honesty, openness, and authenticity, just because the tribe expects you to conform, will only make you more susceptible to "cracking up."

"I gotta hand it to you, Frank.
You always said you wanted to play golf in China!
Looks like you're well on your way now, buddy!"

Chapter 5

Birdman of Altruism

"Trying Softer" means being tender and kind, even when you are damaged.

The first thing Mike told me as he pulled up on his Harley was: "I get along better with animals than I do people."

I wondered if that was a warning. But in spite of his Hell's Angel-like appearance, it didn't feel like it. Instead, I felt an instant connection.

Mike lives life his own way. A short, stocky man in his early 60s, he lives alone and limits his social interactions. He's a good example of why you can't judge a book by its cover. On the outside, Mike looks like a pretty tough character. Everything about him — his appearance, his body language, and his blunt use of language — reveals that he has been through some hard times. Indeed, along his path, he has suffered more than his share of wounds, both physical and psychological.

However, Mike's eyes betray his rough "Don't tread on me!" exterior. They are the eyes of a man who has survived many dark nights of the soul and emerged with deeper wisdom and compassion. It's been my honor to get to know this inspirational man over the past twenty years.

My Interview with Mike

My thanks to Mike for letting me interview him for this book. Though some portions of the dialogue are slightly paraphrased, Mike assured me after reviewing my manuscript that the accounts are essentially accurate.

Me: Can you tell me about your home life, Mike? Didn't you say that your father used to beat you? Was that a regular thing?

Mike: Yeah, man. My ol' man used to beat the hell out of me. Almost every fuckin' day. If I didn't jump when he said jump. Man. Yeah, my stepmother wasn't any different. She used to beat on us too. I joined the fuckin' Marines to get away from him.

Me: How many children were in your family?

Mike: My oldest brother died at two. Then there was my sister. Then my brother who was murdered at Harley. Then me. Then the twins, and my stepsister. There's only four of us kids left now.

Me: You said you all got beat?

Mike: Yeah, but for some reason, my dad always wanted to beat me. So I just told him: "Go ahead, you don't need to abuse my brothers and sisters. Just beat on me."

Me: So you protected your brothers and sisters?

Mike: Yeah. You know, I figured he's gonna beat somebody. Might as well be me.

Me: What were the beatings like?

Mike: Hell, he'd use his fists, his feet, his belt, a 2X4—anything. I have permanent scars on my back. One time a gym teacher asked me if I was being abused at home. He saw all them scars and shit. I said I was in an accident.

Me: So you didn't want to turn your father in?

Mike: No. What's the point? I remember one time he literally hit me over the head with a fryin' pan. I was always havin' concussions. It was a regular thing, man. Then there was that time he kicked me down the cellar steps. I couldn't get up. I had things broken and shit. My father just hollered down "If you can't get up then just live the fuck down there!" I laid there three days, man. My brother had to bring me food and water. I really don't think my ol' man has a conscience."

Me: He's still alive, isn't he?

Mike: Yep. He's 94.

Me: Wasn't he recently in the hospital?

Mike: Yeah, he's out now. I visited him when he was in.

Me: Yes, I remember you were always going in to see him. So you still love your dad?

Mike: Yeah, I love him. But he's one mean sonofabitch. I guess he had a rough life too. He was a hero in WWII. Even had his story written up in magazines and shit. Here's how he is. You know I been outta work for a while. I guarantee if I asked him for five dollars, which I actually did not too long ago, he jus' says "Why don't you go make five fuckin' dollars by workin', yourself!" And, would you believe this: His girlfriend is a fuckin' millionaire!

We talked a little more about his dad. Mike said he thinks his dad had a "Boy named Sue" philosophy. That maybe he thought it was his job to teach his son how to withstand the attacks and brutality of this cruel world. Make him tough. I could tell Mike had thought a lot about why his dad was always so mean, but I could also see he didn't necessarily want to go too much into analyzing his dad in this interview. So I asked him about his military service.

Mike: I joined the Marines to get away from violence! How bout dat shit. I can't talk too much about it, though. I had a Top-Secret Clearance. Basically, I did "special jobs" guarding embassies and shit. I can't talk about it, but you know. I ain't braggin', but I had a lot of combat training.

Me: I respect that you can't go into detail about your military service. Weren't you a champion kickboxer at one point?

Mike: Yeah, man. I was in all kinds of tournaments and shit. I had a bunch of trophies. I sent 'em home to my dad. I probably sent 10 of 'em home. I never saw 'em again. He probably jus' threw 'em in the trash.

Then Mike opened his wallet to show me pictures of himself winning major martial arts competitions. He was obviously highly skilled.

Mike: Because I was good at defending myself—not to brag—but, you know, when I was doing courier work for the government and shit, I didn't need to carry weapons. You know what I mean. I could get around.

I could tell that Mike had participated in many violent situations. He didn't have to say so. It was evident by the things he didn't say. Or couldn't. I had a Top-Secret Security Clearance myself when I was in the service, so I knew what that meant and how it is to be respected. I wasn't going to push him to reveal anything he wouldn't have been comfortable with.

Me: How long were you in the Marines, Mike?

Mike: Five years.

At that point, Mike began to go into more details of some of the combat operations. That's when I turned the tape recorder off. I would never pass on those details.

Mike's military training did not easily translate to civilian life. Unless he wanted to be a mercenary, bouncer or bodyguard, and he wanted no part of those. No. All Mike ever wanted was to have a peaceful, quiet life. "People are fuckin' crazy." He told me many times. "I love animals, man. They don't give you no shit. I love birds, man."

Next, we covered the period of time when he got out of the service and got married. He has one daughter. His marriage didn't work out, but he and his ex parted on good terms. He still sees his daughter. Mike went on to tell me several other things too personal for me to include here. Many too painful.

Mike: One time. You know this restaurant right up here?

Me: Yeah.

Mike: Yeah, one time I met my dad and his girlfriend there for lunch. We were eatin' and shit. And my father said to his girlfriend: "When he was a kid, Mike used to piss out the third-floor window!" He was mockin' me, you know. Then I said: "You forgot to tell her that you locked your children in our bedrooms after school and wouldn't even let us use the bathroom."

Me: I'm sorry you had to go through all that, Mike.

Mike: That's life, man. It is what it is. I'm survivin'.

Me: Tell me more about your love for animals. Isn't there a story where you rescued a baby bird?

Mike: Oh PeeWee! Yeah, man, I loved Peewee! Yeah, man, I was drivin' in town, some back alley. It was a rainy night. I saw two pit bulls splashin' and diggin' in a big puddle. Like they were tryin' to tear somethin' apart. And there was blood, man. I thought it was a squirrel or cat. I really didn't know what it was. I stopped my car. Got out and walked over to the puddle. The dogs ran away. Then this fuckin' bird flies out of the puddle and lands on my shoulder. Those dogs were after this bird, man. Anyway, so I just stood there. And the little guy stayed right there on my shoulder. I talked to it: "So who are you, little guy?" It was a little gray cockatiel. I couldn't believe he just kept sittin' there on my shoulder. I said: "Are you somebody's pet?" Then I opened up both front car doors. He was still on my shoulder. I sat down in the driver's side. I was movin' real slow. I left both car doors open. I said: "What do you want to do, little guy? Now's your chance. Do you want to fly away, or go home with me? It's your choice, buddy."

Me: Then he stayed with you?

Mike: Yeah. I shut the car doors and headed to Walmart to buy him a cage, and food and stuff. PeeWee just sat there on the passenger seat, just ridin' with me like a little buddy. When we got to Walmart, he jumped back up on my shoulder. I walked in the store with him, man, just hangin' out on my shoulder. Some lady came over and told me: "You can't bring your pet in the store." I said: "He ain't my pet." She said: "Well, you still can't bring a bird in here." And I said: "What do you want me to do with him, let him starve? Let him get killed by them pit bulls that were after him?" She walked away. I just went and got this big fuckin' cage and shit and left. Peewee stayed on my shoulder the whole time.

Me: So then you kept him as a pet?

Mike: Oh yeah. I had him for 13 years. I loved PeeWee. A couple of days after I brought him home, though, he got outside and flew away. I stood up on that picnic table. I just looked all around and kept callin' for him. My neighbor told me that usually when that kind of bird flies away, they don't come back. I felt sad, man. I missed him so much. Every day I just stood on the picnic table and kept callin' for him. One day I was standin' out there callin' "PeeWee...PeeWee...." As loud as I could. Then I felt this thud in my chest. He hit me right here, man. It was almost like I'd been shot. It was fuckin' PeeWee, man. He flew right into my chest! I was so glad to see him. I scooped him up, tucked him in my jacket and said: "Glad to have you back, buddy!" I showed you my tattoo of PeeWee, didn't I?

Me: Yeah. Your tattoos are very cool.

Mike then told me about some of the other pets he'd had over the years:

Mike: One time, man, I was comin' in from outside. It was a real cold night, right. And I heard this sound. I couldn't tell what it was. It was like a little squeak or cry. I looked around. I couldn't see anywhere it could have been comin' from. Then I saw this trash can. It had a lid on it. It sounded like the noise was comin' from in the trash can. So I went over, took the lid off. I found this little kitten. All wrapped up in a bloody rag. It was so little. I picked him up. I told him, "I'll take care of you, little buddy." I got an eyedropper and started takin' care of it. I fed it and shit. I took it to work with me every day. I had to so I could feed it every couple of hours. I worked down at the Wirecloth factory, there, you know. My boss came over one day and said: "You can't have a kitten in the workplace." I said, "Who's gonna feed it? Do you want it to fuckin' die? Ok, just put me on leave, fire me or whatever you have to do. I'm takin' care of this cat."

His boss backed off. Mike kept the kitten (Eddie) in a box at his workstation.

Me: Didn't you also have a weasel once? Or a ferret?

Mike: Yeah, man. And I love dogs too. But I couldn't have 'em in the apartments I lived in. And I had a fuckin' black snake, too.

Mike continued: Yeah, when I first found this black snake, I didn't realize he would get so big. When I got him, he wasn't even three feet long. I was at the archery range with my brother when I saw him. I wanted a snake for a pet. So I picked him up. He was only about two feet long. He wrapped himself around my arm. He had about eight inches of his tail hangin' there, and he just kept slappin' my arm with it. Then he bit me in the meaty part of my hand. Man, I had to curl his head to get the fangs out. You know how the teeth are curved. He used to bite. He bit the hell out of me. Finally, he stopped bitin' me, man. I guess he saw I wasn't gonna hurt him. I used to go to this biker bar, man. And I used to take my snake. I called her Shoe Baby. I used to say "Shoe Baby, don't you bite me. And she did stop bitin' me. She grew. I'm not shittin' you, to about eight feet long. She used to hide in our apartment. My wife would say: Don't worry about Shoe Baby, she'll be alright. Then here she'd come glidin' across the living room floor. She'd climb up my leg and come up right in my face and give me a kiss. Anyway, yeah, man, I used to hide my snake under my coat when I went to the bar. She was wrapped all around me and shit. That was cool, man. She was eight fuckin' feet long. And she got along with my weasel. The weasel, his name was Sammy, wanted to attack Shoe Baby, 'cause they are natural enemies in the wild, you know. But I would just look at Sammy and say: "Don't even think about it!" He'd just make a funny noise, look at me and then jump up on the couch with me, my wife and my daughter. My daughter would laugh. Animals are smart, man. They'll listen to you if you love 'em. They really listen to you if their name ends with the "E" sound.

End of Interview

Mike is amazingly non-judgmental. He gives everyone the benefit of the doubt, upon first meeting. He automatically respects people, unless or until they reveal their true colors to be less than honorable. That's when he steps up, with respect and courage, to speak truth to power and hold people accountable for their actions.

For example, one time in Walmart when he was at the checkout counter, Mike witnessed a mother smacking her little girl in the face. The child was barely older than a baby. She could only sit helplessly in the shopping cart while her mother roughed her up and screamed at her. The woman was obviously at the end of her rope.

Without thinking twice, Mike walked over to the lady. "Excuse me, Ma'am, if you hit that child again, I'm callin' 911."

The mother of the sobbing child reacted defensively. In a loud voice, she yelled: "Don't you tell me how to raise my daughter! I'll call 911 myself and have you arrested for harassing me!"

Then a store manager came over. "What's going on?" he asked.

"She was abusing her baby, and I won't stand for that," Mike stated calmly. The woman started arguing and making a scene.

"I'm afraid I'll have to ask you to leave the store," the manager said to Mike.

"Ok," Mike said. He headed for the door. Exiting, he turned around, looked at the abusive mother and said: "Be kind to your child, Ma'am."

Mike is known for his generosity. One hot summer day, a couple of years ago, I saw him wearing a really cool, lightweight hat designed to give the back of your neck shade, as well as your face. At the time, I was spending many of my days working outside at a farm. As soon as I saw his hat, I thought to myself, *Man, that's the kind of hat I need. It would be so much better than the straw one I have.* I casually remarked to Mike about how much I liked his hat. I gave him no indication that I even wanted one like it. Later that day, Mike knocked on my door and gave me his special hat. He had washed it and fully prepared it as a present for me. I was touched by such a kind gesture. I also have several other wonderful and thoughtful gifts Mike has given me, made by Native American friends of his.

The other day, I happened to be visiting a friend of mine. I had stopped in to ask if he would be so kind as to proofread my book. When I told him I have a chapter devoted to Mike, my friend Brian smiled and said: "Did you ever see what Mike gave me?"

"No," I said.

Brian then showed me a little, exotic-looking black dagger. It was very interesting looking, with its own attractive sheath.

"Yeah," Brian said. "One day, Mike was showing me his personal knife collection. We were sitting outside at the picnic table. I could see how fond and proud he was of all of his knives. It really is a very nice collection. He had all kinds of unusual sizes and shapes of knives. I thought they were very cool. I'm sure he appreciated my interest. Well, I really know he appreciated my interest because the next day he gave me this cool little dagger. I didn't know what to say. I just accepted it with gratitude. I know it's one of his favorites. And I don't even know Mike that well."

"He loves to give of himself," I said.

Today, Mike lives a simple life. He likes peace and quiet. After leaving the violence of his gang-affiliated city life, Mike set himself up in a small country apartment with only the bare necessities. He works in a nursing home and loves being kind to the "old people." He helps out in various capacities and makes little more than minimum wage. "I'm doing ok," he always says. "I'm survivin'."

Mike's apartment is one of six in an old converted barn. He is kind and helpful to his neighbors. He pays his rent early and in cash. Though he currently has no pets in his apartment, every day Mike feeds hundreds of birds in various feeders and spots on the property. He can tell you not only the kinds of birds that come around but, in many cases, the personalities of a few of his favorite feathered friends. One of his favorite things in life is listening to their songs and watching the way they interact with each other. Beyond Mike's understanding and compassion for birds, it is obvious he cares deeply about all living creatures, especially the most vulnerable ones.

Mike's old car, which he hand-painted an earthy green, features several bumper stickers. The one on the left side of the trunk says "Don't Tread on Me." The one directly opposite it on the right side of the trunk says "Power to the Peaceful." I can see how each message reflects a strong side of Mike's character.

Mike is a survivor. He has been through more hell then he will tell anyone. No matter how badly anyone treats him, he refuses to go to his attacker's level. By never closing his heart, practicing forgiveness, showing everyone respect—animals as well as people—he has become a hero to me. I recognize Mike as a man of principle and honor. He walks his talk, softly but firmly, honestly and consistently. Eventually, you get used to his "colorful" language.

Mike is not a joiner. He lives on the fringe of society, always minding his own business. He is all too familiar with loss and grief. Not counting his military experiences, he has lost almost all of his family and friends. He may not be traditionally college educated, but he certainly has earned a Ph.D. from the School of Hard Knocks. Life isn't a theoretical proposition to him. It's just real.

Mike is often judged to be everything he is not. When he started his last job, for example, in a home for senior citizens, a few obviously ignorant and insensitive co-workers mocked him when he first got hired. They made fun of him for being so kind to the residents. They also belittled him for being in the military. And these were, supposedly, good caregiving professionals.

I don't think those intimidated by Mike were afraid that he would hurt them in any way physically. Rather, I believe that it was his strength of character that made them uncomfortable. When they looked in the mirror of his example, they probably saw how they couldn't or didn't measure up. Sometimes people not so keen on self-responsibility find it quite unsettling to see someone else demonstrating how vulnerability is strength, and kindness has its own healing power.

Mike embraces a "live and let live" attitude. He considers what others think of him to be none of *his* business. He is confident and content enough to march to his own drummer. His position is that people can think whatever they choose to think. Their opinions are their own to deal with. It's hard not to admire Mike for that, especially when you realize how many times and how many ways he's been beaten down. Mike has grown to the point where he is in no need of trophies, certificates, or any recognition for the daily good deeds he does. Instead, he just follows the dictates of his own tender heart—a heart he is brave enough to reveal regularly.

If anybody understands the difference between force and power, it is Mike. In the military, he was a Special Operations

Warrior with deadly skills. He hints at special operations where his orders were to "clear a building, top to bottom." So he certainly knows what *force* can do. He also knows the *power* of kind-heartedness and vulnerability. He gave his heart to PeeWee one night in a dark alley. Understanding the power of love, he has mastered forgiveness. Mike is happy and healthy today because he chooses to forgive himself, as well as those who have trespassed against him, for any time he might have crossed into dark territory.

The character traits I am describing make Mike a "strong" man. His strength doesn't come from his muscles or skills as a martial artist or combat veteran. What makes Mike strong is that he has nothing to prove. Mike has learned enough about himself to know better than to try too hard at anything. He seems relaxed all the time. He will try hard *enough* at everything. But he's pretty well finished with *trying too hard* at anything.

Mike keeps his heart as well as his mind open and understands what soft power is. He is strong enough to take a baby kitten into a factory full of macho men, and feed it with a doll's baby bottle. He is strong enough to rescue a bird from the jaws of two pit bulls, and take care of it for 13 years. He is strong enough to speak his truth to power whenever he sees an injustice. Most importantly and impressively, Mike is strong enough to show those who have trespassed against him, including his abusive father, the healing power of forgiveness.

After our interview, and after I thanked Mike for being so open, as he was about to leave, he turned and said: "Oh, yeah, did you ever see my flamingo tattoo?"

Halfway out the door, he turned around and stuck his leg back through the door. He then rolled his left pant leg up. Prominently featured on his calf was a large tattoo of a pink flamingo. Then he turned to walk away. With a devilish grin, Mike looked back over his shoulder: "Yeah, I got this to remember my outlaw girlfriend. She was from Florida. Man, she was crazy. One time we was dancing in some bar along Route 30, and her 45 dropped out of her pants! It landed right on the dance floor, man! I kid you not!"

"Ok, Fly! I know you're around here somewhere!"

Chapter 6

Children are the Teachers

"Trying Softer" means forgiving others for the sake of your own heart.

My friend Julie grew up in South Africa. She is a tall, pretty blond woman of Swiss descent. She is in her mid-60s and has a wonderful British accent. I love hearing her speak. She has a very open, animated and refreshingly honest and direct style of relating. When she smiles, her whole being lights up. Neither her spirituality nor her beautiful heart can ever stay hidden.

Julie's mother was a diminutive, soft-spoken, kind and loving woman. Her father was 6'7", strong, severe, imposing and demanding. He could be very cruel. Whenever Julie did not do as her father commanded, he would beat her. Julie loved both of her parents.

When I interviewed Julie for this book, I asked, "You loved your father even though he was so cruel?"

"Yes, I always loved my father, though most of the time, I hated the way he treated me when I was growing up. He put me through hell much of my childhood. Sometimes the pain was unbearable. But I always showed him love and respect. That's just how I am. I thought if I showed him enough love, I could bring it out of him."

Her father had a hard leather whip. It had a handle and then a flat section, like a sharpening strop on a barber chair. It was his torture tool of choice, and the first thing the big man went for whenever he felt his daughter needed to be taught a lesson.

First, he would yank her into her bedroom and position her little body in front of him. He made sure she was shirtless and had her tender back fully exposed to him. Then he would assume a "manly" firm stance to have full swings with his whip. Lash after lash—gash after gash—the blood-stained strop ripped open little Julie's flesh. It took only the smallest things to bring out his rage.

Says Julie: "One of my worst beatings happened because one day I forgot to have my father's cup of tea and newspaper waiting for him by his favorite chair when he returned from work."

For fear of being beaten herself, or worse, Julie's mother could only stand by in horror, listening to her daughter's agonized cries.

"Each time, as soon as the beatings were over, my mother would rush to my aid. She was so loving and so comforting. With her own tears falling onto my face, she would gently lower me into the bathtub filled with healing crystals. The warm baths were always soothing to my back. She always did everything she could to help me heal. She completely enveloped me with love, compassion, and as much comfort as she could provide. At least my father let her do that. My back is permanently scarred from the beatings."

There were some times when Julie and her father got along ok. But he never even tried to hide his disappointment that his firstborn had been a girl. Even though Julie could run faster and jump higher than all of the boys in her age group, her father never attended any of her school sports activities. He took her fishing once in a while. And Julie says he also enjoyed having her help him tend to his beehives. These were rare, treasured moments with her dad.

When she talks about her father's cruel ways of disciplining, you can still see the pain on her face, six decades later. No wonder. She is wonderfully open and honest, totally her authentic self and unafraid to share her most personal experiences.

While the atmosphere of her home life was dark and dangerous, the landscape of South Africa where she grew up was idyllic.

"I loved where we lived," Julie says, the pain on her face melting.

Says Julie: "We had the best food in the world. All we had to do was walk into our backyard, and there would be papayas, mangos and banana trees. Or you could just grab an apple, or a plum, whatever you might be hungry for. And it was all so fresh. We used no pesticides. And the Mediterranean climate was wonderful. We would play on the beaches, run through desert areas and into the most beautiful, lush green forests. Of course, you always had to look up when you walked under a tree to make sure a boa constrictor wasn't waiting to drop down, wrap around you and squeeze the life out of you. And I loved that we always could see beautiful mountains in the distance."

I asked Julie to tell me more about the animals.

"Oh, I love all animals! And we had them all! Yes, we had all of the lions, giraffes, and hippos, as you would imagine. Along with the snakes. And Oh my gosh, the spiders! I hated the spiders! O-o-o-o! Some were as big as your hand. You always had to be alert to your environment. Sometimes a rogue elephant would stomp through a village. It would trample everybody and everything in its way.

Julie continued: "I had an uncle who was part of law enforcement. He would usually be the one called to go and shoot the elephants if they were on a deadly rampage. He was picked to do it because he was such a good shot. But, like me, he loved animals and hated to do it. He especially loved the elephants. He always said the only way he could put one down was because he was saving lives.

"Hippos seemed to cause the most problems. They are very aggressive. If they yawn, watch out. That's a warning. They will attack, and you can't outrun them. They can run close to 40 miles per hour. Sometimes a lion would just creep out of the jungle and grab a child off the playground.

"Those were the natural dangers—just part of life around us. When you grow up among wild animals, you learn to accept these everyday dangers and realities. And you develop a true appreciation for nature and all of God's creatures. I always loved seeing the giraffes. Especially the babies. They are so cute. I do miss the animals. And the fresh food."

When Julie turned 18, she left home. That also meant leaving two younger siblings. All she could do was pray that they would be ok. Once she eventually got her own place, she had them over as much as she could. She was always a caring big sister.

When Julie was 20, she met the love of her life in the church. His name was Jared.

"Jared was actually dating Miss South Africa at the time I met him," Julie says, smiling. "I know it sounds cliché, but he truly was the nicest man in the world, but when I first met Jared, I was a little worried about being with a man, because of my difficult relationship. I could only hope that the same heart I used to love my father in spite of his constant abuse would enable me to give Jared all of the love he so deserved, and I so wanted to give him."

That is exactly what happened. Julie and Jared were totally and completely compatible. She describes Jared as being so wonderfully kind and gentle (the opposite of her harsh and severely abusive father). "Loving Jared was the most natural thing I ever did. In every way, we both knew that we were meant for each other."

Julie and Jared soon married. They set up housekeeping in a beautiful little cottage. They were as happy together as any two people could be. Julie describes their relationship as "perfect." She attributes it all to Jared, describing how he was so loved by everyone. Even Julie's father accepted Jared as a good son-in-law. A year passed. Then Julie and Jared had a baby boy.

The day after the baby was born, while Julie was still in the hospital, her father unexpectedly appeared at the door to her room. Julie was sitting in a chair holding her infant son snugly in a soft blanket.

Staring at his newborn grandson, and with a fierce voice, her cruel father demanded. "Give him to me. He is mine!"

Jared was there also. But he knew that Julie needed to handle this situation herself. She handed the infant to Jared. She stood up slowly. She took a few cautious steps toward the tyrant. Then she stared directly into her giant father's eyes. With soulful fire, fueled by years of pent-up hurt, anger, and resentment, she squared off with her father. Motivated by love, and for every right reason, Julie blasted her father: "No, Dad! He is MY son! You will never touch him! You will never hurt my child!" Roaring her truth, her eyes became as penetrating and resolute as her commanding voice. Engulfed in the loving strength of the fiercely protective and motivated mother she was, Julie boldly declared to her father, and the whole Universe to hear: "My son will know only love!"

No mother ever meant anything so confidently and strongly. Then something amazing happened.

The previously stern, demanding, giant Swiss grandfather was instantly diminished. All of the color drained from his face. Julie says she never saw anyone look so destroyed. "His face got completely white," she says. "I thought he was going to collapse. I couldn't believe I had stood up to him like that. I had never defied any of his wishes before."

It's true. Nobody had ever said "No" with such authority, power and resolve to the big Swiss dictator. Leaving his defenses in a puddle on the hospital floor, the new grandfather and newly unmasked bully lowered his head and quietly walked out of the room.

Three weeks later, Julie and Jared took the baby to her parents' house. It was a surprise visit. Her dad was sitting in his easy chair. Julie brought her baby into the living room.

She walked confidently over to her father. With love on her face and no words spoken, she gently handed her dad his new grandson. This is what Julie recalls about that moment:

"My father held his baby grandson in his big hands, so tenderly. And he began to sob. He lowered his head and began to cry uncontrollably. He cried so hard, I had to take my son back until he could regain his composure. I can't describe the sounds my father made. They were primal and guttural. Sounds I'd actually never heard before. It was like some kind of eruption, expulsion or explosion even, of a lifetime of pain, hurt and sadness. I felt great compassion for him. When he stopped crying, I handed his grandson back to him. And the way my dad cradled my baby was the gentlest thing I ever saw. With his big hands holding this precious little infant, so safely so securely, he just kept gently kissing our little Michael on the forehead. All the while, I could hear him whispering the most loving things anyone could say. It was a major turning point in all our lives. After that day, my father became the perfect, totally loving grandfather — an all-around transformed man. I had always forgiven him. But it took my son being born to allow him to forgive himself."

The dam had broken. Not because anything was forced. It was just the opposite. It was the combined soft power of a mother's love and a baby's innocence that finally brought this tyrant to his knees. No longer could this controlling, brutal and abusive man hide his true nature. Not even from himself. The jig was up. For the first time, probably since he was a child, Julie's father was able to allow his authentic self to emerge. No more hiding his heart behind a tough-guy exterior, no more controlling others to protect himself, no more trying too hard to prove that he was a real man. Such is the power of love. Such is the power of a helpless baby. And such is the power of one's true nature wanting to reveal itself.

So many of us go through our lives trying to be who and how we think we should be rather than accepting how we are when all it does is cause pain. How can it not? It's going against nature. Julie's father was actually a softie on the inside. Deep down, he was a tender-hearted man full of (blocked up) compassion. Probably all of his life, albeit except for the abuse he suffered as a child, all he wanted was to be able to express his tenderness and love for his family. I'm sure he suffered for most of his life, from not being able to show his loving side. He believed that a "real man" had to be strong and a severe disciplinarian — even to the point of committing unspeakable abuse upon his daughter. Once he broke down and collapsed into himself — because of the power of his infant grandson — his real, healthier self was freed.

From then on it was: stand back and watch the healing and forgiveness happen! Julie then, two years later, had a second child, a beautiful daughter. The blossoming family enjoyed an idyllic life.

Every morning, Jared would get up with the kids. They would laugh and play together. He proved to be even more loving than Julie had imagined. He would usually take them outside to a beautiful stream. They would catch fish or frogs while Julie made breakfast. Then they would all eat together before Jared left for work. They were truly a blissfully happy family.

Meanwhile, Julie's parents moved to a country farm. Julie, Jared, and the kids enjoyed going to visit them. The children loved their grandfather as well as their grandmother. Life was good all around.

One typical morning, after breakfast, Jared left for work on his motorcycle. Later that day, about the time he would have been leaving work, Julie remembers that something very strange happened. She was sitting at the kitchen table, when, for no apparent reason, she suddenly felt as if she had been punched in the solar plexus. She almost fainted. Concerned and confused, she made sure to give the kids a quick supper before tending to herself. Then, with her clothes still on, she went into the bedroom to lie down for a few minutes. The next thing Julie knew it was morning. She had blacked out for almost 12 hours. She didn't remember sleeping or dreaming. She got up and groggily picked up the morning paper. The headline read:

"Motorcycle Accident on Diagonal Street"

"I looked at the picture," Julie recounts. "I could see it was a mangled motorcycle. And I could see a covered body lying in the road. I thought to myself, How terrible. I felt compassion for the grieving family. It never occurred to me to associate that picture in the paper with Jared. It wasn't that unusual for him to occasionally work all night."

At that moment, the phone rang. It was a policeman. He asked Julie if she would be home for the next hour. He said he just wanted to speak with her. Julie had no idea why the police wanted to talk to her, but she was willing to help them out. Maybe they thought she could help solve a crime or something. In that part of South Africa, there was a lot of law breaking and violence. Marauding gangs would regularly come into a village to rob innocent people. Often, they would do more than that to the women. It wasn't unusual for a decapitated body to be discovered in an alley or behind some bushes, by an innocent passerby.

Jared will probably be home before the police get here, Julie thought to herself. "Meanwhile, I'd better check on those leftovers," she muttered as she heard a car coming up the lane. As she walked toward the patrol car, two uniformed officers exited the vehicle.

Says Julie: "This is where I don't have much memory. I can remember one of the police officers saying that he had some bad news to tell me. And I remember how he reached around me to keep me from falling. When he told me why he was there, I collapsed. My world had ended. It was the worst thing that could have happened. It couldn't be Jared. How could he be gone? It just couldn't be him. Not my husband. Not the love of my life. Not my true soulmate! He was the best person, partner, and daddy in the world.

"I grieved for a long time. I don't know that I ever stopped. I was so devastated. It was the kind of pain that goes beyond pain. Thank God, I had support from family and friends. Without their love and support, I couldn't have survived. But I knew I had to—for my kids. I was honest with them about everything. I never hid anything from them, even my grief. We grieved together. My son was five, and my daughter was three when Jared was killed. We were all still dealing with the raw emotions of that loss when the next horrible thing happened. It might have been five or six weeks later. I dunno.

"One day, my best friend suggested that I take a break from the children. She said that she and her husband would be glad to watch the kids for a weekend. That seemed a well-timed offer. My friend's husband was a big-time attorney in South Africa. They had lots of money. I knew their marriage wasn't great, but my children knew them well and seemed willing to go for a visit. So that's what we did. I delivered my kids to their home for the weekend. I thought, just for an overnight, it might be good for all of us.

When I went back to pick them up, I noticed my daughter was acting strangely. In time, other people noticed the same thing, so I took her to a psychologist. Without going into details, it was determined that my friend's husband had sexually abused my little girl. I was scared, outraged and deeply worried about my little girl. But even before I could figure out how to handle it, I read something else in the local paper. The article said that a prominent attorney had been "dismembered." Not only his head, but all of his appendages had been cut off by a machete-wielding intruder. It was the same man who had sexually abused my little girl! I didn't know what all that meant or why it happened. I felt bad for his widow; she was still my friend, but of course, I was glad he could never hurt my little girl, or any other child, again.

"I had so many mixed emotions going on around this period that I could barely function. But somehow, I kept it together. I got treatment for my little girl. We all went to therapy. And that really helped. I think she got past it. I believe she has healed.

"Jared's death affected everyone deeply. Next to me, it affected his brother Allen the most. We grieved a lot together. I spent hours and hours trying to console him. This continued for months after Jared was gone. I was counseling Allen even while I could barely deal with my own grief.

"One day, Allen called to ask if I would please come visit him. He said he was really depressed. Understanding his need for support, I hurried to his house. We talked for hours. I tried my best to help him put his brother's death in some kind of perspective, but I could see he was in a really dark place. At one point, I asked to use his bathroom. When I was coming out of the bathroom, I could see into Allen's bedroom. In that instant, I heard a loud blast. I saw Allen flying across the room.

Blood was pouring from him. He landed on the bed. Jared's brother had just shot himself! Right in front of me!

"God help us! I don't know how — it had to be pure adrenaline — but somehow I carried him to the car and drove him to the hospital. He lived for four hours.

"Of course, Allen's family relied on me to make the funeral arrangements. Like a zombie, I just went through the motions.

"Eventually I got back to some kind of semi-normal state. I felt I was on a healing path. That's when I met my second husband, Raymond. We fell in love. It wasn't the same as it was with Jared. I knew nothing would ever be that perfect again. But Ray was very good with the kids, and he treated me kindly. I knew that Jared wasn't coming back, and Ray was a good man, so I agreed to marry him. The kids loved him too. I felt he would be a good father to them. And I knew Jared would want me to move on.

"About a week before my wedding, I was talking to my mother on the phone. She and my father were doing well on their new farm. It was a very nice setting. The buildings all had those thatched roofs, you know. Anyway, we were talking about the wedding. My mother was very excited about attending. Our whole family was starting to feel like there was hope in the air. That maybe we could get on with our lives and find some happiness. All of a sudden, in the middle of our conversation, my mother said. 'I need to go, honey, I see smoke outside. I just want to check and see. I'll call you right back.'

"That was the last time I ever talked to my mom. My father called me an hour later to tell me that my mother had just burned to death in a fire. A gang of marauders had tried to burn my parents out by setting a barn on fire. My mother died trying to save the animals.

"In spite of all his efforts, my father hadn't been able to keep her from running into the burning building. I was in total shock, down and out for the count. We all were. I couldn't believe God was allowing all of this to happen. It was like waking up from one nightmare, only to find out you were experiencing another, and another and another.

"Just as on so many occasions before, everyone turned to me to make all of the funeral arrangements. I was so sick, stunned and numb by all of the deaths. I didn't know how I was going to be able to keep moving forward. My mom was my best friend in the world. She always loved me so much. And always did her best to protect me. Even though my father had changed, I suddenly felt as vulnerable as I always had as a little girl.

"Ray and I kept the wedding date. We knew that's what Mom would have wanted. My father rebuilt the barn and worked the farm by himself. Ray, the kids and I always enjoyed visiting him in the country. My father adjusted amazingly well. He was healthy enough to keep working the farm. He was even supportive and very nurturing toward my new family and me. He truly was a changed man. He spent a lot of time and money fixing up the farm again.

"One day, less than a year later, the phone rang. I answered. It was the police. By then I knew the voice. They were calling to tell me that there had been a shooting. I sat down just in time to hear the news that my father had just been shot. The policeman explained that three young black men had come into dad's house to rob him. He said it was evident that my father had resisted. They could tell by the location of the bullet holes in his body. He was shot three times.

"Once again, I found myself going through the familiar motions of making funeral plans. It was just what I did. At least, I felt some comfort in knowing my father and I had finally been able to develop a healthy, loving relationship. I still miss all of my loved ones so much. The three murderers confessed and were sent to prison.

"On top of all of that, as it turned out, Raymond had me fooled. He became very controlling and abusive. And that's an understatement. Finally, without going into details, I'll just say I was able to divorce him.

"Soon after that, the kids and I moved into my parents' farm. We were only there a day or so when there was a knock at our front door. Looking through the window, I saw three black women standing there. I hesitantly opened the door. 'We are the mothers of the boys who killed your father,' one lady in a bright orange scarf announced. They acted almost like I had been expecting them. 'We are here to help you around the farm. We are sorry for the death of your father. He was a good man. We will do everything we can to make life easier for you.'"

Julie reports that after her initial shock, she welcomed the women into her home. She says they showed her great kindness.

Says Julie: "I became friends with the mothers of my father's killers. I truly fell in love with them. It was a beautiful thing. It was unexpected therapy — heaven sent, I'm sure — that helped me heal from so many traumas. It's hard to explain the levels of forgiveness that we all shared and grew from."

Today Julie lives in the States. She has two sons, a daughter, and several grandchildren. She lives alone and is very happy. Having dedicated her life, heart, and soul to helping others, she works two jobs. Her fulltime job is working during the day with special-needs children at a therapy center. All of the kids, and their families, love her. She exudes understanding and compassion. In the evenings, on a part-time basis, Julie works for a senior-care company, providing in-home care for elderly clients in need of Hospice level care.

Everyone who even comes into contact with Julie describes her as having an amazing personality. She truly knows who she is. Even a life filled with hardship and tragedy did not harden her heart. The opposite is true. Julie accepts all that is, without resistance. She lives in the present with a "Try Softer" approach to accepting all that is. She is confident, at peace with herself, and mind/body/spirit-connected. Her heart is wide open, and she shares her joy with everyone she meets. Julie is a walking testimony to the healing power of forgiveness, gratitude, and love, and certainly one of the most beautiful souls on the planet.

It's your choice: You can try the hard way
Or "Try Softer."

Chapter 7

Against the Wind

"Trying Softer" means being aware that you are always making choices.

Sixteen-year-old Austin and his 14-year-old girlfriend had something they wanted to tell his parents. They walked into the house. His mother greeted them in the kitchen. His father was in the living room in a lounge chair reading the paper.

"Susie's pregnant," Austin said.

His father lowered the paper, looked up for a second and said: "I don't see how you're gonna make it." Then he went back to reading the *Daily Record*.

His mom cried.

That was Austin at 16. On that occasion, he had driven Susie to his house in his own car. It was a 1953 Pontiac (which the men in his family liked to call *pony*-acs) that he had saved up for. He had been working all around town at various jobs since age 11.

Austin grew up in a small town in southeastern Pennsylvania. His family was generally thought of as the town's poor folk. Though they were good, hard-working Christian people whom everybody liked, their house was very small and one of only a few that still did not have indoor plumbing. Austin was ashamed of how he lived. But he wasn't ashamed of where he lived. That's because his house was in a nice location in the center of a town he truly loved. Though he wished he could have, he never invited other kids into his house. In fact, whenever he got on or off the school bus, he pretended he lived in a nearby, nicer home.

The first question I asked Austin when I interviewed him for this chapter was: "Did you feel loved growing up?"

"I guess so," was his answer.

I've known Austin for almost 60 years. I knew his parents as well. I can tell you that while his parents might have been short on education, status, material things, money—even words most of the time—they couldn't have loved their three children more. Austin was the oldest. He had a younger brother and sister.

Austin has many wonderful stories from his childhood. Though he was one of the poorest boys in town, his personality and sense of humor earned him such respect that he easily held the title of the coolest kid in town. We're talking back in the days of the "fabulous fifties." When they weren't in school, Austin and his buddies would run all around their country, Mayberry-like, town. There was no shortage of mischief to get into. But the gang never got into trouble-trouble. You know what I mean. They just did boy stuff, like playing ping pong with handmade, super cool paddles, sneaking into sock hops at the town fire hall, spying on all the girls, camping out in their backyards, and holding "Boys Only" meetings in the abandoned school bus behind Shorty's service station. In their *spare* time, they enjoyed swimming and fishing in the nearby lake and playing baseball and football in vacant lots.

The legend of Austin says that he was shaving by age 10. I don't think anybody doubts that. He was also so strong and husky by that age that whenever he got the football, he would just walk steadfastly toward the goal line. It didn't matter that three or four farm boys, with a combined weight of 300 pounds, were wrapped around his legs. He was always picked first to be on any team.

I'm not describing a superhero here. But he was a cool kid. Good enough to be respected by everyone. Bad enough to cause the town cop to always keep an eye on him.

At age 16, Austin dropped out of school and married Susie. They had a beautiful baby boy. They named him Danny. Austin went to work in retail. Hard work came naturally to him, and he provided well for his new family. They even bought a mobile home.

That's how he was going to do it, Dad!

Like so many of our buddies at that time, Austin got drafted and was sent to Viet Nam. He proved himself a leader in every aspect of the service, including combat. In November 1967 he was wounded in a seven-day battle, known as the Battle of the Trapezoid. He came home with a chest full of medals and a purple heart. To this day, Austin never goes anywhere without his purple heart in his pocket. He carried it to help him whenever he had to face problems. It gave him strength at every step or stage of his life, in every situation.

After returning from Viet Nam and recovering from his physical battle wounds, Austin rallied against the war. Even while people were disrespecting our returning vets, some even spitting on our soldiers, Austin remained respectful. He became a strong voice for non-violence. "I considered draft dodgers to be casualties of the war too," he says.

While he was in the Army, he passed his high school equivalency exam. That enabled him to get better jobs. He soon found himself managing men's clothing stores in several states. Primarily he worked for one company that sent him to different locations.

By this time in my story, I should tell you that Austin has quite a distinctive look about him. I think "distinguished" would be fair to say. He has always been both image- and fashion-conscious. After the service, he grew a beard. But not just any ol' scraggly set of whiskers. No. Austin's beard was, literally, a prize-winning enhancement on his face. A face so intense that more than one person has approached him to seriously inquire: "Excuse me, sir, are you a warlock?" To some people, I guess, his long hair and thick beard gave him enough mystique to stimulate their imaginations.

Austin's job kept him apart from his wife and son, often for months at a time. They decided to divorce. Soon after that, and after a lot of soul-searching, Austin made another decision. He committed to finding out what gifts he had and to doing something contributory with his life. He wanted to make a difference, especially in the lives of young people. He enrolled in college. This was something unheard of in his family, so, of course, they were all very proud and supportive.

Just before starting college, Austin remarried. His new wife was a teacher. Austin felt the same calling, so he majored in education. Eventually, by working part-time and taking as many credits as possible at school, Austin not only got his bachelor's degree, but he went on to get a master's degree in psychology, plus 21 credits beyond that. He even earned a principal's certificate. He went from high school dropout to graduating magna cum laude — straight A's in graduate school.

After graduation, Austin taught elementary school for five years. He earned the title of head teacher. Soon after that accomplishment, he accepted an offer to become the principal of two small elementary schools. By this time, he and his second wife had divorced, and Austin had married again. His new wife, Bev, was also an elementary school teacher. They were, and still are, totally in love and compatible enough to go the distance. She is as amazing and inspirational as he is.

As most people understand, and certainly all service men and women know, soldiers who have seen combat come home with some form of PTSD. Austin was no exception. After Viet Nam, and probably because of it, Austin developed a drinking problem. Most people never knew because he was always more than functional. He drank only at home in the evenings, never during the day. But it was a serious dependency that would get worse as the years passed. It took lots of heavy whiskey to dim haunting memories from the jungles of Southeast Asia.

After Austin had been a principal for about five years, and because he had done so many positive, innovative things, he was offered the position of being the principal of two larger schools. It would mean a larger salary plus a lot more responsibility. Austin happily accepted the new position. Before he could even digest what all the promotion would mean, he received devastating news from his eye doctor. He was diagnosed with an inherited disease called Leber's Optic Neuropathy. It is a rare kind of incurable — and (to date) irreversible — chronic inflammation of the optic nerve. Austin was going to go blind.

His first response was to go out and buy a talking clock.

When the school board learned of Austin's condition, they wanted to help him with his adjustment. They offered to raise his salary, but allow him to remain at the two smaller schools. They understood that, once he lost his vision, he would know his way around better. Austin thanked the board for their kind offer but said he was excited and dedicated to following through on the original plan. He wanted to go where he was most needed.

When the matter of Austin's blindness, and whether he would be able to handle the bigger schools and increased responsibility, came up before the school board, they unanimously agreed to grant his wish to take over the larger schools. The president of the school board reportedly said to the district superintendent: "If anybody can do it, Austin can." Everyone agreed. Austin took the new position to help more children.

"Hearing that statement of confidence," Austin said, "did more to prepare me for the new position than any training or device I could have received."

Knowing that it was only a matter of months until he would lose almost all of his sight, Austin did everything he could to prepare. Not that going blind is anything you can prepare for.

"The only blind person I had ever really noticed was that guy who sat at the front gate of the York Fair. I remember him sitting there holding a tin cup for money, with his German shepherd," Austin said. "I was hoping I could do better, but it was good to know I had that to fall back on," Austin quipped, showing his healthy and ever-present sense of humor.

Of course, the same Austin who always carried the football and half of the other team's players across the line and into the end zone was not going to settle for squatting at a carnival with a tin cup. No. And knowing him as I do, it's easy to understand why he was not going to give up on his dreams. That's because Austin never met a challenge he didn't love to face. He calls it the "rebel" in him.

"I like breaking stereotypes and proving people wrong," he says. "My dad saying: 'I don't know how you're gonna do it,' was all I needed to hear to make sure I did it. I've always, I guess, been able to find motivation whenever I needed it."

Knowing that a tsunami of darkness and disorientation was inescapably headed his way, Austin asked his loving wife to take him on *beauty rides*. At that point, a beauty ride to Austin meant getting in the car and literally going anywhere. There were no sights that weren't magnificent. If he saw a thistle, a rock, or a dead piece of wood, he recognized them all as breathtaking.

Austin and his wife went to many special places, such as Longwood Gardens, so that he could store up fresh memories. He attended theater presentations, visited museums, even read a couple of books he'd always wanted to read. They watched kids playing on the playground. They took their dogs to the dog park and visited the zoo. Bev even took her husband to a strip club. They shared many memorable rides through the Amish countryside that Austin so loves. They held each other during sunsets and sunrises. They went to the ocean.

Austin didn't miss anything. All the things that we take for granted, like the bark on a tree, reflections in a puddle, cloud formations, cows in a field, the color of dirt — the colors of *anything* — he beheld in all its glory. The sun! Wow! Just to see the sunshine! What a miracle! What could be more glorious! How precious life is.

In addition to taking in all the sights he could — most importantly, looking at the faces of his loved ones — Austin connected with various agencies for the blind. He went to special classes to help him learn Braille and to prepare in other ways. He was tutored on how to use various technological aids. And at school, he hired reader aids to work with him in the evenings, whom he paid out of his own pocket.

At first, his left eye went dark. That came fairly quickly. Then, over a period of a few months, he gradually lost the vision in his right eye. By that time, Austin had memorized his way around his schools. He had also memorized the names of each student in both of his schools. He faced this incredible challenge with the same acceptance and courage that he faced each combat mission in Viet Nam.

When he was talking to me about this chapter, Austin asked me to check out a country song by George Jones. The song is called "Choices." It starts out like this:

I've had choices
Since the day that I was born
There were voices
That told me right from wrong...

"At each turn of my life," Austin told me, "I've always been aware that I have choices. In my early marriage, we could have chosen abortion. Instead of traveling with my job, I could have stayed with Susie and Danny. Instead of going into the service, I could have dodged the draft. And I guided myself through my part in the Viet Nam war with choices.

"Choices whether or not to stay in a failing marriage. Choices about drinking or not. The choice, once I knew the sight-loss was coming, to take the job with even more challenges and responsibility. Even the choice to become a principal in the first place, rather than just continue on and get my doctorate. I feel like if you're looking for a thread in my life or a theme that guided me, it is that I've always known I have choices. And I've always been willing to take responsibility for the consequences of those choices."

When I asked Austin what his parents thought of all of his choices, he replied:

"I'm sure they were proud of me. You know how my father was a man of few words. When I was in Viet Nam, I got the one and only letter he ever sent me. He was writing to tell me four things: 1) He'd heard of the death of another boy from our town. 2) There would be a car waiting for me when I returned. 3) To tell me: 'Keep your head down.' And 4) he was proud of me for making sergeant. He signed it, 'Love, Dad.'

Austin went on for fifteen years, as not just a blind principal of two large schools, but an exceptional principal. He received numerous awards, even a letter from President Clinton, praising his achievements. Because I was his friend through all of these transitions, I know how much he loved his students. And his teachers. He especially appreciated his personal aides and office staff. And they all loved him. Austin was inspirational in every way. He developed a wonderful reputation in his community, even statewide.

You won't be surprised to hear that Austin's retirement dinner was a big deal. It wasn't just a bunch of faculty members holding a banquet for him at a fire hall. It was the event of the year held at a fine restaurant. The evening's event was billed as "Reflections." There were 125 people in attendance. Everybody from school officials to the janitorial staff, to fellow teachers and principals, to family and even dear friends (myself included).

There were speeches and jokes and accounts of all of Austin's innovations. There were parents of students giving testimony to how much he had helped their kids. A scholarship was set up in Austin's name and honor. It was a well-deserved, grand tribute to one of the best principals anywhere in the country.

Typical of Austin, he punctuated the whole evening with his impromptu humor. Known for his self-deprecating jokes, all through the evening and with perfect timing, Austin lobbed out hilarious one-liners. When the official part of the retirement dinner had concluded, the DJ (one of Austin's janitors) started up the dance music. Austin hit the dance floor. I saw him dancing with three women. The first song of the evening was "Glory Days" by Bruce Springsteen. Quite appropriate, I thought.

One story Austin told at the retirement dinner was about the time in the hall when he stopped to ask the janitor's vacuum cleaner how his day was going. Austin knew there was something upright in front of him, but the janitor was nowhere near his parked sweeper.

Another story that came up during the dinner was anything but funny. It's a poignant account of something that happened when Austin first became an elementary school principal and still had normal vision. Back then, he had no reason even to suspect that he would ever have any kind of eye problem.

One morning, around 10:00, Austin was walking through the hall at one of his schools. When he turned a corner, he noticed his art teacher standing outside his classroom. The students were still in the room and the door was closed. "Hi, Dick, is everything OK?" Austin asked.

The distressed teacher looked up and began sobbing. "My eyes! My eyes are bleeding. I thought I could make it through the day but..."

Austin reached out and hugged his teacher friend. He had been aware that Dick had type-one diabetes, so he understood. Austin arranged for a substitute teacher for the rest of the day. He sent Dick home to take care of himself, reminding his friend: "Don't worry about anything here at school. I've got you covered."

To this day, his art teacher, and great friend, still talks about how compassionate and understanding Austin was, on that occasion and many others.

"How ironic it is that only a month after an incident where he comforted me because of my eye problems, it was Austin who got the unexpected diagnosis that he was going blind," Dick says.

"As you know," Austin said as I was interviewing him, "my retirement dinner wasn't a 'roast' like you see on TV where they hurl insults back and forth. I believe it was funny and enjoyable, yet very tasteful. Not that I had a hand in orchestrating it. I thank dear Bev for that, for all of her hard work. And my staff. It was a wonderful night."

"Yes, it was," I said. "And you were so funny that night. You made everybody feel so relaxed. And you were very humble in the midst of all of those compliments. It was perfect."

"As you know, humor has been what keeps me sane."

Soon after Austin retired, he received an eight-page letter from his son, Danny. Danny had earned his doctorate in marine biology and was already a well-known scientist. He was married and had a son, "little" Austin. The letter informed Austin that Danny had always felt that his true gender was female. He said he was going to have a sex change operation. As Austin had never suspected any such issue, he was completely surprised and shocked.

I remember that period. I read Danny's letter too. It was a letter reflecting such courage, such self-respect, and such love. I was floored by it. "Floored" meaning I just wanted to support him in every way. And that was Austin's reaction too.

I asked Austin during this interview: "When you first received that letter from your son Danny revealing that he was going to transition into Danielle, how did you feel?"

"Love," Austin said. "I just felt love. I called him. We had probably a five-hour phone conversation. Then Bev and I went to see him the next day. We talked on his patio for another five or six hours. Of course, I was totally supportive. My only concern was the operation itself, for his health. But he is a scientist and he explained it all. As you remember, the whole transformation took years."

So Blam! Blam! Blam! Throughout his life, instead of trying too hard and denying the issues he faced or fighting straight against them, Austin remained flexible and adaptive. As each challenge came his way, he found, not just *a* way to "use" his circumstances to grow, but always *the best* way. His history, his pattern, and the reason I am including him in this book has been to continuously "Try Softer" enough to gain more and more self-knowledge. The second part of *his way* then has always been to use that increased self-awareness, self-understanding, and self-knowledge to help others. That is what self-responsibility is all about.

Austin's son, Danny (now daughter, Danielle) had made it clear in his eight-page letter that his gender identity crisis had almost caused him to take his own life. He had been trying hard for 40 years to pretend that he was a well-adjusted man. Since his earliest years, on the inside, Danny had known he was essentially female. It wasn't until he "Tried Softer," surrendered to the truth of his identity, and had the operation that he (now she) was able to move forward as a happy and productive marine biologist. She is doing invaluable work for our environment.

Throughout his life, Austin never started anything he didn't finish. He had Danny when he was a boy himself. They didn't spend much time together in the early years. But in the end, Austin was there for his only child when love counted the most.

Likewise, with his Viet Nam experiences. Austin didn't just go to war, come home and bury the horrible memories. He went to serve his country, did so with valor, came home and then spoke the truth of his heart and conscience to power. He respectfully and bravely stood against the war. In time, after about 25 years, Austin decided to face his Viet Nam experiences head-on. He continued to drink as a way of numbing the pain, but he knew that in order to heal from his PTSD, he would eventually have to face his wartime pain. He began researching and contacting his fellow combat veterans. He finally was able to organize a reunion of 15 of his buddies, and their wives and sweethearts. They had all served with him, including his commanding officer. He invited them to his home.

They came in from all parts of the country. This time, unlike when, as a boy, he was too embarrassed even to admit where he lived, Principal Austin—Blind Austin—Soldier Austin—Veteran Austin—Courageous Austin was proud to invite his combat brothers to his beautiful home. His guests had three full bathrooms to choose from. All indoors. Austin hosted these Viet Nam combat vet reunions several years in a row. He keeps in touch with all of them.

Austin was on a roll. He was "trying softer" at every turn. All that was left was to face his alcohol addiction. He knew with all his being that this final challenge wasn't going to be easy. He started attending a regular, weekly PTSD counseling group for combat veterans. Bev would usually drop him off at the counseling center. Then I would pick him up. After the group meeting, I would drive us to a restaurant called The Paddock. Bev would then join us later for a bite to eat. Then she would take Austin home. We planned it so Austin and I would get to the restaurant a half hour or so before Bev. That allowed Austin and me to process his always intense session. Knowing him so well, I was usually able to help him de-brief and relax. The thing about those PTSD meetings that bothered Austin the most was that his brothers in arms were on him constantly about his drinking. While that was a good, right and healthy thing, of course, it caused Austin to become very defensive. His body was used to drinking high volumes of whiskey for probably, at that point, 30 years; he wasn't about to give that up.

"I don't have my sight. I'm retired. I'm dependent on everybody for everything," he'd say. "I don't know if I even want to give up drinking. It's like my smoking. I know it's not good for me, but damn, it's hard to give up these things I've always done."

After about six months of counseling, Austin stopped going. The pressure on him to quit drinking was only making him want to drink more. He was in terrible distress. But here we go again: One day Austin decided to face his alcohol addiction head-on. Just like he does everything. He told Bev he wanted to be admitted to the hospital for detox.

He was admitted. And Thank God he was! Because the process of getting alcohol out of his system almost killed him. He was in and out of intensive care many times. He has no memory of a year of his life. It was touch and go for almost the whole year.

I knew he was in the hospital, and I wanted to visit. But Bev said: "Austin won't know who you are. He is so weak and delusional. He doesn't even know where he is most of the time. Sometimes he thinks a nurse is me, or that I am one of his nurses."

It was rough going. But Austin being Austin, he hung in there. Finally, he was allowed to come home. He was already disoriented enough from the blindness. When he got home, he was even more disoriented from the ordeal of detoxification. When he fell down a flight of steps, after two weeks, everyone was horrified, but no one was surprised.

Austin was rushed to the hospital. He had obviously banged his head hard. He didn't break any bones, but he did have a brain swelling issue. He was operated on and a shunt was installed to relieve swelling. Today, aside from age-appropriate aches and pains and a little arthritis in his knees, he is in good health. His blindness has degenerated from having 5% sight, mostly peripheral, to total blindness. That's because glaucoma has set in, on top of the other disease.

Yet he is back to his old self. When I talk to him, his memory is excellent, his humor is bright and well-timed, his heart is more open than ever, and he continues to be a wise counselor to all who know him.

I haven't gotten him to admit it yet fully, but I think since he lost his sight, he is a better listener. When you are talking to him, you feel like he is listening with the full attention of his heart. He never complains about anything. When he does talk about his inability to see anything, he refers to "the blindness." The blindness isn't who he is, nor does it define him. It's just one of many things he has to navigate every day. He is not religious in the traditional sense of belonging to any one congregation or prayer group. Rather, he is a genuinely spiritual man who honors all religions. Every night when he gets into bed, the first thing Austin does is thank God for his many blessings.

Among his blessings are many friends. I am proud and honored to be one of his closest. He has taught me much about myself. Whenever I think I am having a bad day—maybe I have a fever blister or a hangnail—I think of Austin. Then I close my eyes for just a few seconds to get a glimpse of the dark world he lives in 24/7. That puts it in perspective. He is amazing.

Austin's story, like others in this book, is certainly an inspiring one. But of course, we can find other, more dramatic and extreme, accounts of people doing impossible things— such as the guy who cut off his own arm to free himself from being trapped in a rocky crevice. My point in including these particular stories is to show that you don't have to look far and wide to find amazingly courageous and inspirational people. They don't all make the news. For this book, all I needed to do is look to my left, then look to my right, to recognize the everyday struggles of "ordinary" friends already in my life.

If you want to locate a hero, it's easy. Just look in the mirror. You are a hero. So are your friends and your neighbors. We all face uniquely difficult challenges we are not sure we can overcome. Until we do. Each of us has a unique purpose and mission, and an opportunity to discover our authentic selves by peeling away the fear-based blocks from within.

Life is about facing the circumstances we manifest, co-orchestrated by the Universe and our own choices and perceptions. You are as inspirational as anyone. Only you know how difficult your life has been and what you've had to do and contend with to keep going. And you do. You keep going and growing. That's why you are reading this book. We all seek the same thing: we want to learn how to love and be loved. And ultimately, that's a "Try Softer" journey.

Austin must have told me a hundred times, in the course of our long friendship, that his theme song was "Against the Wind." In talking with him about this book, I asked him what "Try Softer" means to him. He said it means going with the flow. It means facing reality and not trying to force things to change, rather seeking the best possible outcome you can find by being flexible. He said it's like the old adage: "When life gives you lemons, make lemonade."

Well, life has certainly given Austin some lemons. And he turned them all into that special kind of *aid* that continues to enhance the lives of everyone he has touched.

Austin has been retired for over 20 years now. He and Bev have a beautiful home on 12 acres in the country. These days he is happiest just hanging out with his three dogs. Over the years, he's had many dogs, always at least one. For several years now, he and Bev have been rescuing English mastiffs.

Whenever he does venture out, Austin invariably runs into a former student or teacher of his, from his days as a principal. They always have wonderful compliments to extend to him. Most recently, Austin's wife was in the store when approached by a woman she didn't recognize. The lady asked Bev if she would please relay to Austin that all seven of her kids were in school when Austin was the principal. "My kids always said that your husband had magic powers!" she said. "They all really respected him."

In case you are thinking that the blindness has put Austin in a permanent rocking chair, you must not have been paying attention to my description of him. When he first retired, for about 10 years or so, though legally blind, he still had about 5% peripheral vision. Hardly enough to call it "vision," but he was able to vaguely make out some contrasting objects, such as the location of a building or a tree. One time he "saw" what he assumed was a stick. When he went to pick it up, the snake slithered away.

For many years, he kept taking care of things around their large property. He built huge stone border walls, mowed many acres, maintained walking paths through his woods (for people and deer alike), developed a fish pond, did snow removal, even occasionally used a chainsaw. But the shade kept coming down. Soon that cherished 5% diminished to total darkness. What did Austin do then? Well, of course, that's when he took up watercolor painting!

I helped him get started by lining up the right supplies — brushes, paints, and some good 300-pound cold-pressed watercolor paper. With a little assistance from his wife, he created several very powerful and poignant paintings featuring images from his Viet Nam experiences.

Austin continues to take care of all his daily business. He is amazingly independent. His mastery of technology, especially machines and devices designed to help the visually impaired, makes it possible for him to do many things even sighted people have a hard time keeping up with.

Of course, Austin has slowed down a bit. I can't say he hasn't. He'll soon be 73 years old. But he's still the coolest kid in town. He is enjoying life as a wonderful husband, father, grandfather, friend, community leader, and dog whisperer. Oh, and don't go to visit him if you don't want to hear loud music (could be country, could be rock) blasting from his state-of-the-art speakers, while he dances with that magic grin of his.

Finally, to wrap up the interview, I asked Austin: "Let's say you die, and you are able to somehow still be at your funeral. You know, like you are invisible or something. What is the thing you would *most* like to hear someone say about you?"

Austin didn't ponder long. "I think he moved!"

Think back to the Japanese parable at the beginning of this book. What if Austin, as a little boy, had traveled to the top school district in the country with the goal of someday becoming the Best School Principal in the land? Think of all the learning and changes and challenges he had to go through to reach his goal. For Austin, who always led with his heart, rather than his ego, it was never about: "How hard must I try to get there fast?" It was always about: "How can I try soft enough to allow the best version of myself to help as many people as possible?"

Austin has a tin cup. He uses it to hold water when he is painting.

Chapter 8

Live Your Own Life

"Trying Softer means accepting that you are part of the sea of humanity - the ocean in a drop of water."

D o you sometimes feel misunderstood, isolated and out of step with others? Like you're the only one who can't seem to get his act together? These are common concerns. Many of us feel that if we would dare to reveal our *real* selves to the world, we would be painfully judged.

Each of us is born with a particular purpose and mission. No matter who you are — no matter how cut off from the world you feel — a "Try Softer" approach to life will enable you to blossom into increasingly better "versions" of yourself. But first, you need to reconnect with the human race. You need to know that you are really not as strange, different and isolated from everyone else as you think you are.

What is Most Personal is Most General.

Most of us would be afraid or embarrassed to expose our innermost secrets to anyone. We are sure that the weird, sick, and painful thoughts, feelings, behaviors and memories we carry around in our inner *vaults*, are unlike anyone else's. Yet, the truth is you are not as different from the rest of us as you think. While your particular gifts are unique to your personality, path, and purpose, every question in your psyche or concern of your heart is shared by over seven billion people.

There are that many pieces to the human puzzle. But none are the exact shape as you.

To the extent you can allow your "authentic self" to blossom into the full puzzle piece you are meant to contribute, you will be happy and healthy. To the extent you keep the "real you" hidden, you will create disharmony and ill health. That's because nothing is more difficult in life than going against your own nature. You might as well try rolling a boulder up Mt. Everest. Every time you try to hide, block, deny or in any way fool your true self, you create distress. If you do it too much, and for too long, you are bound to create some form of disease. **"Trying Softer" is the key to living a fulfilled life. It is the natural way to become your healthiest self.**

The quest for self-actualization requires us to balance our egos, remove our social masks, and live from our hearts. Adopting a non-judgmental *live-and-let-live* attitude is a challenge for many of us. Our egos often get in the way of our hearts. The rewards, however, for allowing yourself to be real — honest, whole, healthy and compassionate — are grander than words can describe. In the final analysis, we're all in the same boat.

Of the over seven billion people on the planet: Who among us isn't...

- Wanting and needing intimacy, yet often afraid of closeness and feeling vulnerable?

- Trying to speak their truth, yet sometimes concealing their most authentic voice because of shame, self-doubt, guilt, fear or judgment?

- Searching for happiness in other places, people or things, knowing all the while that it can come only from within?

- Afraid to care for themselves first, for fear of being thought of as selfish?

- Pretending not to hear their own Heart Song, the sweetest sound in their universe, for fear of the risks they might have to take to "sing" it?

- Trying to get "ahead" without an understanding of what?

- Afraid if their real self were exposed, the rest of the world would abandon them?

- Struggling with as many issues around success as around failure?

- Holding themselves back by their own interpretation of their past and/or fearful projections into the future?

- Sensing all the time, at least in some vague or indescribable way, that they are a Child of God, of Spirit, of the Universe, of Life and Love, and yet somewhat mystified or confused about religion and spirituality?

- Feeling guilty, at least on some occasions, for accepting too much abundance?

- Regretful in their heart when they inflict pain on another?

- Concerned much of the time about being "right"?

- In awe of the *weakness* and vulnerability of a baby, and yet humbled by its *strength* and power?

- At times amazed at their own capacity to feel contradictory emotions such as — happy and sad, good and bad, strong and weak, healthy and sick, secure and frightened, confident and confused — all at the same time?

- Creating their own reality through their beliefs, choices, and perceptions, yet at the same time feeling like a victim?

- Often trying to convince others of the very thing they themselves doubt the most?

- At least a little bit mystified by sex?

- Wondering in the back of their mind whether they are living the life they are meant to?

- Curious about the relationship between free will and destiny?

- Apt to tell a lie on occasion to protect themselves or others?

- Sometimes lulled into a feeling of just passively going along with life, as if it is just some kind of unimportant dress rehearsal?

- Tempted at times to blame others for something that they know they are responsible for?

- Afraid to reveal the strange side of themselves — the side they think is weird — and admit things that others might consider are crazy? Things such as... perhaps you actually did see a UFO... or a ghost... or felt the presence of a departed loved one?

- Doing things sometimes in an effort to conform to the tribe, to conceal their own personal power?

- Longing to cry out, "Hey, world, look at me? Please acknowledge my uniqueness. I count! I matter! Please see me! Hear me! Please celebrate with me the fact that there has never been anyone like me in the Universe. Nor will there ever be again!"

Are you really so different from the rest of us?

"Knowing others is Intelligence; knowing yourself is wisdom."
—Lao-tzu

The gift of free will gives us the power to be choice makers. Each day, according to informed guesses, we make over 30,000 decisions. Each choice we make is either in the direction of growing into greater alignment or blocking our most authentic selves. Every decision carries risk. And that's a good thing. If you take a chance, step out of your comfort zone and discover it works, then you have gained self-knowledge. If it doesn't work, you have gained wisdom. Not taking a risk can be the biggest risk of all.

Easy does it.

Along my journey, I've been blessed to have many opportunities to help others. Professional areas I've worked in include: special education teacher, probation officer, family therapist, psychotherapist, martial arts instructor, artist, and author. All the while, just being a father and grandfather blessed with a beautiful family and lots of friends has brought me the greatest joy.

Ralph Waldo Emerson suggests: "Adopt the pace of nature: her secret is patience."

Like the boy in the parable, we often want to go straight to the reward and skip the process. You know how it is. Why delay gratification?

Let's get this thing done... Let's get it over with... C'mon, let's get this show on the road! Give me my prize!

Isn't it true? You just want to get that room painted! Why waste time messing with any protective tape or drop cloths? Preparation-smeperation!!

You want bright, shiny teeth, but don't want to bother brushing, flossing and maintaining healthy eating habits. You want to change your body image, but don't want to change your lifestyle.

You get the picture. Impatience is a way of life for many of us. We live in the era of instant gratification. God forbid it takes more than two seconds to pull up a website on our computers. Sooner or later, we all discover that when it comes to accomplishing greater goals such as establishing happy and healthy relationships, finding a job you love, and being a successful parent, we can't make things happen ahead of their time. We need to "try softly" enough to allow inner blocks to be released.

Sometimes even natural motivators can inhibit our success. Qualities we love, if overdone—such as exuberance, excitement, passion, and romanticism—can diminish our patience and persistence.

To achieve most goals, we need to keep our emotions balanced. For example, athletes such as football players obviously need to be passionate and fired up about defeating their opponents. Otherwise, they probably won't win. But they can't afford to get so excited that they forget the rules of the game or how to play the positions they are assigned to. The same is true for anyone attempting to perform a highly skilled task, even professional singers or dancers. To share their gifts with the world, talented individuals need to love what they do. All the while, however, they need to maintain enough composure, mind/body/spirit control, and centeredness to achieve success. If the young boy in the parable had not been passionate about his dream, he wouldn't have been able to summon the energy to travel across Japan to the master's dojo.

Once we learn how to be our authentic selves, we can honor, respect, and embrace every ounce of passion and desire we have. Trying too hard will create more problems and blocks to our happiness. No matter what your psychological block consists of—whether it is impatience, arrogance, ignorance, laziness, inadequate time constraints, excess passion or excitement, lack of caring or concern, fear of failure or whatever—you will keep sabotaging your own efforts until you "Try Softer."

Time to Wake Up

The wisdom of the master in the karate parable is a valuable reminder that to get from point A to goal Z, we have to grow ourselves along the way. We can do this only by slowing down, accepting everything about ourselves exactly as we are. That is when we are most open to learning. Important keys to conscious living, learning, and growing include:

Self-awareness: means realizing where you are, what you are doing, and how you are thinking and feeling in each moment.

Self-understanding: requires knowing your strengths and weaknesses, including talents and limitations.

Self-discipline: embraces the ability to make yourself do things in your own best interest, even when you feel no motivation to do so.

Energy focus: means being able to channel your energy effectively.

How to Increase Self-Awareness

Do you go through your day automatically? At the day's end, do you find yourself wondering what happened to the time? Maybe you can't even remember all of the things you did during the day. Well, join the club. In many ways, to one degree or another, we are all *hypnotized, mesmerized, dazed, conditioned, programmed and controlled.* Especially in today's world of excessive stimulation. Stimulation and information overload come to us in all forms, and from all kinds of sources. Consider: 24-hour news reports, constant political discourse, sophisticated advertising, addictive social media conversations, and continuous messages from the internet in general. Excessive stimuli vying for our attention, both from the environment and within ourselves, are enough to put anyone in a daze.

I'm not saying that these things are bad or harmful. Nor am I suggesting that a world with less interactive communication, and information availability, would be a better one. Although I must confess, I often long for the simpler days of my childhood, where if you wanted to call a friend, you dialed the operator from your house phone and said, "Hi, Marge, this is Tom. Would you please connect me with Marie Waterson?" She would do that as soon as others on your same "party line" finished their conversations.

And if you wanted to know what was happening in the world, you would just read the evening paper or watch the one-and-only nightly news segment in front of your 9-inch, black and white TV set. Then of course, if you were a kid, you would go back out and play until dark. That's when your dad or mom would holler from the porch, or whistle, as in my father's case, for you to come home.

The 1950s were called the "fabulous fifties" for a good reason. Certainly not for everybody, such as lower-income, inner-city residents, or many people of color, but for most Americans the pace of life back then was slower and less stressed. I believe that kind of lifestyle made it easier for everyone to develop a fuller sense of self-awareness. As a kid, I always felt that I knew who I was and what I was doing. As you'll read, a couple of chapters ahead, I was busy being "Superman."

Self-awareness means paying attention to yourself — to what you are thinking, saying and doing. If your life is like a merry-go-round or hamster wheel, it's not easy to stay centered and self-aware.

Self-aware means being conscious of what motivates you to behave as you do. The best way to increase your self-awareness is to slow yourself down and focus on your breathing, even if only for one or two times a day.

Another thing that is helpful is to start paying attention to how you use your body. That means recognizing how you are feeling throughout the day. It also means listening for and accepting any and all feedback from others about how you affect them. Also, when you look in the mirror, take an extra minute actually to see the person looking back at you. It won't hurt you to stare at that handsome mug or beautiful face a tad longer. The last tip is to listen to your internal dialogue. Begin to pay attention to what and all you are thinking. Is your self-talk good, fun and healthy? Or is it harmful and self-defeating? These are some elements of your life to begin becoming aware of.

How to increase Self-Understanding

Even if you don't know it or you want to deny it, you actually do understand yourself. If you don't, who does? No one else lives in your skin suit. No other person is "inner sanctum" privy to your particular set of personal qualities, likes and dislikes, strengths and weaknesses, talents and abilities. Others may recognize your attributes when you display them, but no one can really know what makes you tick, better than yourself.

You can know someone else only to the extent you understand yourself. That's because understanding one human being well — the one you are closest to (yourself) — enables you to gain a natural appreciation and understanding of the general psychology of all humans. Of course, better understanding between and among human beings facilitates more cooperation and harmony in the world.

More often than not, we learn about ourselves the hard way. Our human tendency is to find out what we like and don't like by trial and error. That's normal self-exploration. But you can also come to better know and learn about who you really are, what your preferences and aptitudes are, by paying attention to the lives of others. For example, if you see your father constantly battling depression, anger, feelings of failure and having an inability to maintain healthy relationships because of his alcohol addiction, then you can learn that you don't want to be that way. We have a world of role models to demonstrate ways we want to be, and ways we definitely do not want to emulate.

How to improve Self-Discipline

Unless you are already a highly self-motivated individual, you will probably need the assistance of others to help you break a pattern of procrastination, inertia, or even what you might think of as laziness. It comes down to how badly you want what you want. In some cases, when we know what we want and think we can't live without, we can become militaristically disciplined. When fired up to that extreme about accomplishing a task or reaching a goal, we can almost transform ourselves into unstoppable robots — doing whatever we need to do to achieve our goal. More often, there are things we might sort of want to do or have, but it's OK if we don't cross the finish line. Life goes on — whatever.

To become more self-disciplined, you need to understand why that is a good goal for you. It helps to remind yourself of all the ways you will be better off if you commit to becoming more self-directed.

Regarding the Japanese karate parable, the boy certainly didn't sound lazy or unwilling to work hard. The problem wasn't that he lacked motivation. The problem was that he was motivated by the wrong thing, his ego.

"Trying Softer" does not mean doing nothing. Nor does it mean not doing your best or being 100% proactive. Rather, it means doing everything you can to release blocks to your own success. It is work of a spiritual nature. It is the art of knowing how to try just hard enough, without crossing into counterproductive territory. Being lazy isn't "Trying Softer."

There is nothing lazy about a baby. A baby is fully tuned in and motivated to experience all of life all of the time. All a child wants to do is explore the world. Motivation is not usually an issue for a kid.

For the rest of us, however, once we know it is advantageous if not life-saving to kick our willpower into gear — such as when the morbidly obese person wants to lose weight — we often need the help of others.

For example, I know for myself — who probably was a bit of a slacker as a teenager — that going into the military taught me a lot about self-discipline. Hey, all it took to get my ass in gear was the entire military complex of the United States. The point is, we all need help from others.

You know what I'm saying. People who want to get healthier, for example, often find it helpful to join a diet program or hire a life coach to keep them on point. Don't be afraid to ask your significant other to help you break a habit or make whatever changes you desire. You really can do anything you put your mind to. Ultimately, as already discussed, you are the captain of your own destiny. To finally convince yourself that nothing will get done until or unless you do it turns out to be a healthy and helpful action. That, and remembering that "Life is Short." It's true that today is the first day of the rest of your life. It's also true that today might be your last day on Earth.

How to improve Energy Focus

Nothing takes place without energy. Many physicists contend that energy is all that exists in the Universe. Scientists say that all material forms such as a table, a flower, a tree, a car, a rock or anything you can think of, including a person — including you — are just energy dances in various forms. Perhaps the most critical area where the focus of our energy makes the most significant difference is in what we choose to think. My involvement in the martial arts helped clarify that lesson for me.

Proper karate training strengthens all aspects of personality. It does so by putting you in challenging situations wherein you have to face yourself as you actually are. With no place to hide, you must accomplish what is required of you to defend yourself. The main benefit of being in that kind of stressful, yet structured, setting is that it teaches you that every challenge you face is, first and foremost, an opportunity to learn more about yourself. And you definitely need to learn what makes you tick in the dojo. Having enough self-knowledge can mean the difference between dodging a punch and getting your block knocked off. Such personal insight automatically translates to everyday life.

Revisiting our Japanese parable, we don't know what the boy decided to do. Perhaps he considered the master's reply to be nothing but dream-squelching and problematic:

"This is crazy! I had no idea that the harder I try to reach my goal, the longer it will take me. Well, there's no use me trying to tame this fire of desire within me. I'll be constantly frustrated. Rather than spend the next 30-plus years here, I might as well forget it. I don't have that kind of patience. By the time I completed training, I'd be as old as the master is now!"

Or the boy could have recognized the master's reply to be an opportunity far greater than he ever hoped for:

"Wow! This is wonderful news! I get it! I needed to hear such wisdom. Thank you, kind master. I understand now that I can not only reach my goal in probably less than 12 years simply by "trying softer," but bigger than that and way more important than that, I see now how I will grow me into the best version of myself in the process! Like a sponge, I am ready to absorb all of the master's wisdom. I am ready, willing and able to relax into the whole growth process now. It will lead to wherever it leads."

Can you imagine a student knocking on the door of a medical school and asking how soon she could become the world's best doctor? I'm sure it's happened. In theory, of course, the dream of becoming a great physician is a noble, generous and inspirational goal for anyone. But think of the tremendous personal growth and the universe of academic knowledge and learning that needs to be absorbed for any student to self-actualize into such a great doctor.

Everything we do both requires and inspires us to keep growing and learning. An ordinary trip to the grocery store, for example, takes intelligence, competence, awareness, and focus. You have to be present and have your wits about you to do anything. When you become preoccupied with fighting parts of yourself, your ability to function effectively is inhibited. Sometimes you can get so out of kilter it would be like trying to move your car down the road by pushing on the gas pedal and the brake at the same time. Like cars, people need to be fully aligned and in good condition to move forward effectively.

Seven signs you are trying too hard

1) You feel "put upon" by your relationships.

If you feel like you give more than you receive in your relationships, you are probably trying too hard to please others. "Try Softer" to allow yourself to have more faith in the strength, quality and amount of love in your relationships. Let go of expectations regarding how others "should" be. Try saying "no" more often, when it is how you feel.

2) You are over-extended.

If all you do is spend your life running from one obligation to another, you do everybody a disservice, including yourself. Sooner or later you will burn out. It's better to slow down before that happens. Look for ways to "Try Softer" during the day. You may be able to accomplish this by eliminating certain tasks and consolidating others. Realize that when you just go through the motions of your life at breakneck speed, you are just stuck in a fast-paced habit. Through consciousness of choice, you can readjust your lifestyle, take a breath, and remember to build in some "me time" each day.

3) You keep comparing yourself to others.

Comparing yourself to others is just a roundabout way of looking for reasons to demean or diminish yourself. Putting yourself down is a kind of self-punishment you don't need. It doesn't help you or anyone else. Putting others down to build yourself up (because you feel inferior, to begin with) is also a futile attempt to feel better about yourself. Instead of comparing yourself to others, "Try Softer" to examine the you of yesterday compared to the you of today. Recognize that your uniqueness is at the heart of what makes you a one-of-a-kind gem in the treasure chest of humanity. You are supposed to have the nose you have, be as tall as you are, have the shape, size, skin color, laugh, walk and unique perspective on life that you have. Those components that make you the unique, one-of-a-kind, once-in-the-Universe individual that you are.

4) Your best is never good enough.

It takes a healthy attitude and a good work ethic to want to do a good job at whatever you do. At the heart of that intention is a desire to help everyone as much as you can. But if your self-imposed standards of achievement are too high, not only are you setting yourself up to feel like a failure, even when you are successful, you will ultimately lose your incentive to do anything. "Try Softer" by reminding yourself that success is as much in the process as it is in the end result. The truth is, no one can ever do better than their best. Cut yourself some slack. If you operate from an old tape in your head from childhood that says you can never be good enough, replace that negative loop with one that says you are always good enough. You are still doing the best you can with the information you have.

5) You are a people pleaser.

Always seeking the approval of others is also a remnant of unmet childhood needs. The "Try Softer" antidote to seeking validation from others is to turn the spotlight more inward, and start recognizing your own strengths. It's not easy to break the conditioned habit of caring too much about what others think. It might help you to realize the truth that you are not on their minds as much as you think. The "Try Softer" way is to put less energy into worrying about how others see you and more focus on feeling better about yourself.

6) You are obsessed with your kids' success.

We all want our kids to succeed at what they do. Nothing ultimately matters more to us than their happiness. The "Try Softer" way to guide them and help them along their journey to a healthy, happy adulthood is to support, nurture and encourage them at each stage. The most helpful thing is to model success in your own life. I'm not talking about success regarding money in the bank, but rather success in being a happy, healthy person yourself. When you push or pressure your children to do more than they can at the stage where they are, or be further along in their development — especially to please you — you may be setting them up for a lifetime of self-sabotaging behaviors. "Trying Softer" is all about balance. Love and support your kids unconditionally and with all your heart, but respect them enough to allow them to make the mistakes they need to make along the way.

7) You never give yourself downtime.

Do you feel guilty relaxing and not doing anything constructive? Would you believe that relaxing is probably the most constructive thing you can ever do? Again, it's a matter of balance. It is not only an unhealthy thing to not allow yourself to relax and rest, but it's also really a form of self-abuse. Consider changing your self-talk so that what you repeat to yourself becomes more self-affirming and supportive. Fashion thoughts like: "I could really use a timeout. I've certainly earned a little bit of 'me time' to recharge my batteries. Everybody will benefit if I learn to relax more. That's because I'll be happier and healthier. Plus, when I do engage in productive activities, I'll be that much better and more effective."

"Trying softer" means being fully present.

What helps the most is to keep your mind in the present moment. Worrying about the past or being too eager to get to some future place of recognition inhibits the flow of all things in your best interest. Sit down, relax and put your attention on your breathing. Even if you do this for only 20 seconds, you will feel yourself to be more alive in the present moment. The healthiest, "softest" thing to do — meaning the thing requiring the least effort — is to literally do "No-thing." *Relax...relax... relax.* Allow your beautiful self to *just* BE. Wow! What a Great Gift to give to yourself.

"Knowing yourself is the beginning of all wisdom."
— Aristotle

Chapter 9

Candles in the Dojo

"Trying Softer" means finding balance — mind/body and spirit.

Karate is about relax...relax...relax...*and then BOOM! TOTAL FOCUS!* You don't punch with your arms. You punch with your hips. You don't kick with your legs. You kick with your hips. That is where the power comes from. In the martial arts, it's all about the contrast between hard and soft, fast and slow, relaxing and tensing as you allow your natural body mechanics to work for you.

The same principles of body mechanics apply to your golf swing. How far the ball goes depends on how hard it is hit. How hard you hit it depends on the speed of your swing. The speed of your swing largely depends on how relaxed and correctly positioned you are as you rotate your hips with proper timing. Whether it's golf, karate, tennis, swinging a bat, in almost any sport, to be successful, you need to relax and let body mechanics work for you. And of course, no matter what the sport or physical activity is, proper breathing is always crucial. You can't relax if your breathing is too fast or too shallow.

Having people tell you that relaxing is the key to becoming a better martial artist is one thing. Being in karate and learning the truth of that via blood, sweat, and tears is something else. Essentially, the master's cautionary advice to the Japanese boy in the parable was that: "To become proficient in the martial arts, you must not try too hard."

The same wisdom applies outside of the dojo. "Trying Softer" is the key to improving every area of your life. My karate experiences helped me better understand that. What follows is a glimpse of some of the experiences and lessons I learned in karate. Things I learned not "in theory," but rather by participating mind/body/spirit for many years.

After returning from Viet Nam and earning his black belt, my brother Randy opened his own karate school. This was around 1976. His dojo was a spiritual place of self-discovery and healing as much as it was a traditional workout environment. At that time, I was working for the county as a probation officer and family therapist. I thought it would be a good way to stay in shape, so I joined his first class of white belts.

The only thing I knew about karate was the stories I'd heard about my brother's own training. They were crazy stories like running through the snow barefoot, kicking and punching till your limbs felt like rubber, regularly pushing workouts until some student faints, not to mention all the while having to (literally) fend off nips and scratches from his sensei's pet lion cub. I was surprised, myself, that I didn't let those tidbits of information dissuade me from joining his school. I had just enough confidence to embark on what would prove to be a wonderful journey of self-discovery.

I was a social worker at the time. I felt I probably understood a little about people. I knew I was ready, willing and able to learn more about myself. Acquiring self-knowledge has always been the strongest motivating force within me. Plus, experiences such as serving in the military, graduating from college, being married, and being a father had opened both my eyes and my heart to life in general. Looking back, it's easy to see how the stage was set for me to dive into the mystery of karate. I soon discovered that I was going to have to face an opponent more formidable than a full-grown lion. I was going to have to face myself.

To build a solid martial arts foundation, we started each class by reviewing the basics. We constantly practiced all of the fundamental stances, techniques, and movements. It wasn't unusual for a new student to spend three months of training just learning how to make a fist. Learning karate is like learning a new language. You need to learn the alphabet first. You have to learn how to construct words before you can *say* anything.

Being the sensei's brother turned out not to be a position of special treatment. If anything, I had to work harder than the other students. I respected completely my brother's guidance. I wouldn't have expected him to treat me any other way. He was, and still is, a great teacher of mine.

After 10 years of dedicated study, and a fair amount of blood, sweat, and tears, I earned my black belt. What an honor and privilege and, I admit, a respectable accomplishment. I spent the next 10 years then co-instructing with my sensei-brother.

The cardinal rule in our school was summed up in just one word: RESPECT. That meant respect for yourself, your fellow trainees, the dojo, and of course, the teachers. It also meant that we expected our students to represent themselves as mature ladies and gentlemen full of kindness, courtesy, and respect for everyone, outside of class. We expected our karatekas to develop and maintain absolute respect for all of life.

The true Karate Way, as our school interpreted it was The Way of "Trying Softer." We taught our students:

There is no such thing as a first attack.

Karate begins and ends with Respect.

Our style of martial arts reflected the legacy of Sensei Ginchin Funakoshi - 1868 to 1957, whose core message to his students could be paraphrased as

"No matter how you may excel in the art of karate, and in your scholastic endeavors, nothing is more important than your behavior and your humility as observed in daily life."

Concerning our affiliation with other schools, we competed now and then in tournaments, demonstrations, that kind of thing. But that was the exception rather than the rule. For the most part, we humbly kept to ourselves. We were kind of a side path enclave of Funakoshi devotees.

Our students were a mixed group of dedicated men and women ranging in age from around five to 75. We taught teachers, preachers, children, educators, police officers, factory workers, business people, even an occasional physician. We especially loved accommodating people with special needs.

Though our school stayed rather non-competitive, we honored and respected every school's unique way of accomplishing the primary goal and purpose of karate, which is Character Development.

To help our karatekas gain a deeper understanding of their own attitudes, my brother and I developed a variety of therapeutic avenues. We developed innovative training exercises designed to help our students get to know themselves better. The training strategies combined elements of the martial arts with psychology.

For example: If a student had an anger management problem, we might have them modify bunkai (the understanding of a particular block or attack) by visualizing their opponent as the embodiment of their own anger. That way, in their imagination, every time they punched, kicked, or threw down their opponent, they were prevailing over their own anger. Every time they avoided or blocked an attack, they were keeping their "problem" from getting the best of them.

More generally, along those same lines, we would often instruct our students, as they were moving back and forth across the dojo executing combinations of blocks and attacks, to focus on defeating personal weaknesses or problem areas such as pride, fear, arrogance, procrastination, low self-esteem, depression or anxiety. The key for the students was to visualize some chosen aspect of their character to be strengthened and then imagine that negative trait or tendency to be defeated by their execution of karate movements. The same technique would apply if the trainee chose to focus on larger societal concerns such as poverty, disease, domestic violence, world hunger, and war.

The result was fascinating. To the extent students visualized their opponent as a fault, or negative habit they wanted to eliminate or grow beyond, rather than picturing some imaginary bully or brute out to do them harm, they were able to gain valuable insight into their own personalities.

By participating in such a process of imagination and visualization, incorporated with traditional karate movements, our students learned the underlying truth of karate (and perhaps all of life), which was something Master Funakoshi constantly reminded his students:

"Rather than physical technique, mental technique."

The most common problem we had with every student was trying too hard. At all times, we encouraged mental as well as physical relaxation. We taught various methods of quiet breathing exercises and meditation to help them learn to "talk." Our purpose was to construct circumstances that would allow all karatekas to get in touch with the deepest part of their essential selves—the inner calm of their soul. The part of yourself that I refer to as the Master Within.

These combined mind/body/spirit training exercises enabled our students to take integrated and proactive steps toward helping themselves become more how they wanted to be. As instructors, we always felt that anytime we were able to help students channel their energy in the direction of the enhancement of their character, we were successful.

There were many nights after a good workout when we would all sit in a candlelit circle and openly share thoughts and feelings. While the issues discussed were mostly about karate, our students always took away problem-solving strategies outside the dojo. I guess you could say we had our own version of karate therapy going on. We used karate exercises as healing metaphors for life's daily challenges. A lot of openness and sharing occurred, with great appreciation and respect for everyone's differences.

My brother and I were fully aware that some of our teaching methods were a little off of the traditional karate path. We often wondered what Master Funakoshi might say about our use of psychology and therapeutic growth strategies. In the long run, and for the following reasons, we felt justified and thankful for staying with our innovative style of martial arts instruction:

1) We never let any creative, self-growth exercise interfere with our baseline approach of always having a rigorous, traditional, physical workout. Whether practicing basic drills, katas, kumite, weapons or free-form exercises, we constantly maintained a crisp focus on the most important details of body mechanics. We embraced, honored and always applied Funakoshi's fundamental reminders to keep our stances low and to use our hips to generate power.

2) The more our students invested their minds and imaginations into the workouts, along with the hard-to-avoid blood, sweat, and tears, the deeper their commitment became not only to learn karate, but to foster their own personal growth. Several of our black belts shared with us, later and gratefully, that if we had taught only the physical side of the martial arts, they probably would not have been able to stick it out.

3) Our students, commonly and consistently, reported that the lessons they learned in the dojo better prepared them to deal with life's challenges outside of class. The consensus was that our mind/body/spirit methods of training made karate personal and practical, and helped our karatekas to become more comfortable with their authentic selves. What more useful self-defense posture can there be than a solid measure of self-knowledge and self-awareness? We were also told that our methods of "making us think" actually made the workouts harder. All of our black belt achievers learned not only the benefits of relaxing the total self, mind/body/spirit, but the necessity of "trying softer" to gain maximum success.

4) Most importantly, and without arrogance, my brother and I taught the way we did out of the deepest respect for Master Funakoshi. We always strived to honor all that we believed he stood for.

Regarding karate knowledge, we never became so presumptuous as to think that we knew anything beyond just the tip of the iceberg. That is true even though my brother's sensei trained in Japan, which made our martial arts lineage fairly pure in the sense that we were only a few teachers away from Sensei Funakoshi. We were very proud of such a solid connection with tradition. And we felt highly honored that it afforded us good standing in the Japan Karate Association.

It was out of humility rather than arrogance that my brother and I felt we understood the heart of karate well enough to introduce some of our own teaching methods. We respected and did our best to preserve traditional karate with the same fervor an honest man might feel toward his religion. Never compromising Funakoshi's principles was our first duty, responsibility and rule. The master himself, whose portrait was always displayed in an honored position in our dojo, offered the following about how karate would and should change with the times:

"Hoping to see karate included in the universal physical education taught in our public schools, I set about revising the kata to make them as simple as possible. Times change, the world changes, and obviously martial arts must change too.

"The ultimate aim of karate lies not in victory or defeat, but in the perfection of its participants."

I can't imagine where I'd be today if not for karate. Everything I learned in class, first as a student then as a teacher, has made me a happier, healthier person today. I'm sure I have more confidence and self-discipline for having participated in the martial arts. In managing chi, and knowing when and how to direct energy in all circumstances, my karate training has proven invaluable. I find myself constantly, and naturally, thinking about opposite energies all the time: hard and soft, relaxation and tension, pushing and pulling, moving into or moving away from situations, both real and imagined. Blocks and attacks have become wonderful metaphorical growth tools that I consciously use to help me better address even the most ordinary challenges. And I meditate every day.

While I certainly wouldn't claim to have any more wisdom than anyone else, I must admit that most of the time, I do feel a deep sense of understanding and fulfillment, as per Lao-tzu's reminder to us that:

"Knowing others is Intelligence; knowing yourself is Wisdom."

My Parallel Pony Parable

As a young boy, I traveled around our small town, sometimes in a stroller or carried by my mother. Often in cowboy boots, skipping, or on my pogo stick, bouncing.

I was granted a compassionate ear by most everyone I came into contact with—from my parents, to the minister, to the local cop, to all of my friends and fellow townspeople, including a couple of hobos.

"What is it you wish for, Tommy?" everyone would ask.

"I want a pony. How long will it take me to get one?" I would reply.

"Well, you'll just have to try and win one," my parents consistently offered, letting me know that we couldn't afford one, had no place to keep one, and the odds of me winning anything were slim to none.

"What if I pray for a pony?" I would ask. "Then how long will it take for me to get one?"

"That is up to God," most people would say.

Hmmm, I thought to myself, does that mean it could be tomorrow or could be never? I don't think they know what they are talking about.

I decided to direct my questions straight to the Source, bypassing everybody else. This is what God said to me then, and continues to remind me of every day:

"All of your dreams have already come true, Tommy. Your pony is on her way. All you need to do is relax into acceptance of your truest self, and have faith in Life and Love."

And so I did.

"C'mon, Dynomite. The clock is ticking. All we need to do now
is gallop to the finish line."

Chapter 10

Drawing on Faith

"Trying Softer" means trusting your deepest desires.

A s a little boy growing up in a small, rural town in Pennsylvania, I remember identifying with Superman. I felt totally connected to everything. Six decades later, I can still feel the thrill of running through the grass with a towel pinned around my neck. I was sure if I ran fast enough I could fly.

My Pony Story

"I'm using the rug, Mom," I hollered, trying to stomp the snow from my boots. There was no reply. I closed the back door and sock-skated across the kitchen floor. As I slid into the living room, I caught my mom quickly ending a phone call. The look on her face stopped me in my tracks. Could it be?

"I won the pony, didn't I?" I blurted out. Though Mom couldn't speak, her teary eyes answered me. From that moment on, and for reasons you'll soon understand, I would never be able to ignore the deepest messages from my soul.

A few weeks earlier, I had entered a TV contest to win a pony. It was offered on my favorite show, *Popeye Theater*. The show was hosted by Sally Starr, or "our gal Sal," as she was lovingly called by her many loyal fans. During the '50s and '60s, her show was a major hit with kids in the Philadelphia area.

Sally was one pretty cowgirl, especially from a 10-year-old boy's perspective. Her long blond ponytail, bright smile, and colorful fringed outfits made her a dazzling sight, even when she wasn't leading a local parade on her spirited palomino. She seemed even more beautiful in spirit. People of all ages appreciated her mature and loving personality and great sense of humor. Speaking from her heart, Sally provided sound moral guidance for her young viewers. She was like everyone's favorite aunt or big sister.

Popeye Theater was aired in Philadelphia every weekday at 4:00 p.m., following Dick Clark's Bandstand (later known as *American Bandstand*), filmed in the adjacent studio. I never missed either show, especially Sally's live, two-hour broadcast. Besides her regularly featured sidekick, Chief Halftown, other frequent guests included Gene Autry, Roy Rogers, Colonel Sanders, Dick Clark, and the Three Stooges. Between celebrity appearances and skits, Sally offered cartoons and TV episodes such as *The Lone Ranger*, and *Popeye*. She also promoted products like Good and Plenty, Cocoa Marsh, and Gino's Hamburgers, a favorite fast-food restaurant before the days of McDonald's.

Sally opened each show by saying: "Hope you feel as good as you look, 'cause you sure look good to your gal Sal." She closed every show with "May the Good Lord be blessing you and your family. Bye for now!"

The beginning of my pony story

By the age of six, all around my little town of Oxford, Pennsylvania, I was mainly known for my bright red hair and my love of horses. I couldn't do anything about my hair color or the occasional teasing it brought me, but when horses became the subject, I held my own as a self-proclaimed buckaroo. My parents used to tell their friends. "I don't know about this kid; he eats, breathes, sleeps and dreams about horses." That was definitely the case.

I collected model horse figurines, read horse stories, and went to every horse show I could. I even remember doing paint-by-number horse portraits and hanging them around my room. Whenever my parents took me to a carnival or county fair, I'd be in line for the pony rides before the car door closed. There was little doubt in anybody's mind that, more than anything else, I wanted a pony.

There was a problem, however. Our family of five lived in a small two-bedroom apartment and was in no position to afford even a kitten. Dad worked hard at the furniture factory during the day and spent his evenings doing upholstering for extra money. Mom's fulltime job was staying home with my two younger brothers and me. And yet, my parents continually offered their blessings as I entered contest after contest to make my pony dream come true. Their loving support of my dream-quest validated a central part of who I was becoming.

A Personal Brand of Luck

The rules for how to win the pony, in this latest contest, stated that each contestant was required to make a cattlebrand out of his or her initials. Upon hearing that, I could hardly contain my enthusiasm. As fast as I could, I gathered paper and pencils and sequestered myself in my room.

"Aren't you gonna watch *Howdy Doody*?" my younger brother Randy yelled through our bedroom door.

"No, just leave me alone. I'm gonna win us a pony!" I hollered back.

"Okay, but stay off my bed!"

I knew this project was going to take all of the brain power I could muster. Hmm… How can I arrange my initials T-A-N?

Suddenly I realized that the "A" could become a horseshoe if I rounded it off and widened the top. That was a good start, I thought. But I couldn't figure out what to do with the "T" and the "N." So I went out to the garage where Dad was reupholstering a chair. I didn't really want to interrupt him, but I knew he was great at thinking outside the box. I held up my preliminary sketch and explained my idea. "I don't know what to do with the 'T' and 'N,'" I said to my father.

"Well, let's see," he replied. After a long pause and a few more strikes on the chair with his tack hammer, my dad then said the magic words: "Maybe the 'N' could be stretched out to look like lightning."

That did it! I rushed back to the drawing board and finished up the perfect brand. I mailed it straight off to the good folks at WFIL-TV in Philadelphia. I knew it would win.

The call Mom had tried to hide from me that wintry day had been from the TV station. While I was on my way home from school, a studio representative informed her that my brand had indeed been selected the winner. Mom practically fainted. When the fog cleared, she heard the voice on the other end of the phone say, "Oh and ma'am, you're not required to accept the pony. We'd be happy to give your son a new bicycle instead."

As tempting as that offer must have sounded to her, my dear mother managed to squeak out the words that would change our lives forever: "You don't understand. I cannot tell

I named it: The Lightning-T-Horseshoe

my son that he won a bicycle. That's just not possible. We will — eternal pause — take the pony. Thank you."

As if Mom wasn't already in deep shock, the studio representative then asked her if she would please keep it a secret (from ME!) that I had won the pony. He added that Sally thought it might be fun to have me brought to the studio under the pretense that I had been selected to be in a commercial for Bosco. That way I would be surprised to win my pony on a live broadcast. Yeah…fat chance that was going to happen.

So…it was all of *that* that I saw on Mom's face the second she hung up the phone. She might as well have said, "Hi, Tommy, that was the Holy Grail Delivery Service. As you know, your pony will arrive soon."

A few days later, with baby Larry bundled snuggly, our family piled into the car. Before even turning the key, Dad cocked his head around to warn Randy and me about fighting on the ride ahead. Then he planted a cigar in his mouth, pressed on the gas and aimed the ol' Chevy toward the City of Brotherly Love.

Weaving our way through Amish country and past beautiful old stone farmhouses and buildings of the Brandywine Valley,

I found myself wondering how I was going to act surprised. As if she had read my thoughts, Mom looked back over the seat. "It'll be okay if you can't act surprised today. That was just something the people at the station thought would be fun. But don't worry about it. They'll understand."

Not more then 10 seconds after we had pulled into a visitor's parking space behind the station, an old blue pickup truck pulled in right beside us. Through the wooden side railings, I could see what the truck hauled. There on a bed of straw stood a little brown pony with a blond mane and tail, all tacked up with a red saddle and bridle.

"There's our pony, Randy!" I blurted out.

While leaving the car, Dad said, "We don't know for sure that this one is yours, son. Let's just go inside and see what they want us to do."

While walking toward a door that said Studio C, I whispered to my brother. "That's our pony, Randy."

We knocked and a kind man let us in. "You folks are just in time. I'm headed to the Starr show myself. We just finished taping *Bandstand* and are about to set up for Sally."

So there I was. At the same time that Dick Clark was helping to give birth to American Rock and Roll, I was literally next door giving birth to my fondest dream.

Just before airing, Sally greeted us. She thanked me for agreeing to help her do a commercial. She assured me it would be easy and that she would tell me exactly what to do and when to do it. I nodded yes. Then she gestured toward chairs off to the side of the set and asked our family to sit. I'm sure each of us had our own version of that deer-caught-in-the-headlights look as we waited for the show to begin.

The next thing I knew, Sally was leading my pony, red saddle and all, to a spot in front of the cameras. Then she motioned for me to come on-stage. I felt both shy and ready to explode with excitement. She handed me the reins and directed me to look toward the camera. Then she held up the drawing of my brand and announced to the whole wide world that I was the winner of the cattlebrand contest.

"Here's your pony, Tommy," she said.

My cowgirl angel then shook my hand and invited me to climb into the saddle. Cameras still rolling, I took my seat in what felt like Heaven. I tried to act cool, but inside I was completely overwhelmed. At one point, I remember glancing beyond the lights and cameras toward where my family sat. There was Mom, with baby Larry in her arms, and Dad and Randy too, all standing and clapping. For some reason, I was surprised by how proud they all looked. I knew I had to be at that moment the happiest boy in the world.

Bringing my Pony Home

Thanks to the willingness of my parents to facilitate their son's dream-come-true, and a bunch of amazing (non)coincidences, we were able to make all the necessary accommodations for our beautiful Shetland. We even found the perfect little barn to keep her in. Of course, it just happened to be located right beside my father's workplace.

Like a Hollywood script, everything went fine for several months. My brother and I, as well as our friends, rode Lucky all the time. I loved sharing her with everybody. And, thinking back… I recall a little less teasing about my red hair.

One morning we received an urgent phone call from the caretaker at the barn.

"Ed, you need to get out here right away!"

"What's wrong, Fred?" Dad asked.

"Just hurry. This is something you have to see for yourself."

Not knowing what to expect, our whole family scrambled into the car and headed to our pony. Ten minutes later we were in the barn and rushing to Lucky's stall. I was relieved to see that she was still there, looking fine. However, she was not there alone! A wet and wobbly baby stood by her side, leaning against her for support. I had won a pregnant pony! My dream had come true—two-foaled!

My brother Randy, of course, was even more excited than I by the arrival of this second—no doubt his—pony. But sadly, from the first moment we saw the newborn foal, it didn't appear healthy. Its eyes looked sick and cloudy, and it seemed to be hanging its head. Then when a veterinarian arrived, Dad asked Randy and me to leave for a while. Before we had a chance to understand the situation, the baby pony was pronounced dead.

Devastated, with tears flowing, my brave eight-year-old brother made his version of a grave marker from scrap lumber. Dad, Randy and I dug in silence for an hour before burying Lucky's baby next to a row of pine trees behind the barn. Then Randy sobbed his goodbyes aloud as he hammered his makeshift cross into the ground.

The death of Lucky's baby affected my relationship with Randy in a positive way. Until that incident, I hadn't thought twice about getting mad at him and jumping on him like a tough big brother. Even on the ride to Philly to get my pony, I'm sure I launched a stealth punch or two across that invisible mid-line boundary in the back seat. Truly not mean-spirited at all, but still…I was the king of the hill, big 10-year-old brother on his way to get his pony.

Seeing Lucky's baby be born and then die on the same day was a sad thing. Watching my little brother's dream born and buried on the same day was something else, something deeper and more significant. It made my heart ache in new ways. I suddenly had the painful awareness that my dream had come true in the context of a family. I wasn't the only kid in the world. And I wasn't the only dreamer in the world. I could see, and feel, how my little brother was as devastated by the loss of his pony as I had been elated by winning mine. I realized that my dream coming true had now brought him profound grief.

Though I didn't always know how to show it, I felt more compassion for Randy after that. Whether it came to me as sympathy, empathy, pity or just an older sibling's concern for his younger cowboy partner, I knew it was brotherly love.

Time soothed our grief and life kept unfolding. As seasons changed around us, we had great fun riding our pony through fields and grassy meadows, down country lanes, across streams and even through parking lots in town. I can still see little Randy riding with his favorite boots and coon-skin hat. Those real-life "Happy Days" continued for about two years. Then one evening Dad announced that we would have to move because he had accepted a new job in a nearby city. He said we'd have to sell Lucky.

Now it was my turn to be devastated. I had expected to take care of my pony for the rest of her life. She was my dream come true.

Everyone knew how hard it was for me to sell my pony, especially my parents. How they handled the situation is a testament to their individual characters as well as their love for me. They promised me that when we were settled in our new home, I could get a horse. They kept their word. Within six months of moving, and thanks to Dad's promotion, my brother and I were riding happily through new fields on our beautiful roan-colored Tennessee walking horse.

Looking back on my Pony Quest, it is clear to me that if I had chosen self-defeating thoughts such as, I will never be able to beat the odds and win a pony…or my parents can't afford to keep a pony…or I am not creative enough to form a cattlebrand out of my initials, I would have blocked my pony from coming into my life.

I don't believe luck was involved. I don't believe that God ignored my prayers and just rolled the dice and a pony just happened to come my way. Instead, I see perfect orchestration at every turn. By allowing the Universe to be my booking agent, honoring my deepest desires and acting on them creatively and with love, one thing led to the next. Life unfolded in my best interest. Thankfully, I didn't allow myself to block my dream from coming true. Rather, I tried just softly enough to allow it to happen.

As a child, I was always nurtured and supported. I felt respected. Such unconditional parental love enabled me to allow life's currents to flow through me. I didn't need to block anything for fear of being hurt. I was aware of everything I thought and felt. And because I was appreciated for being my unique self, I had no reason not to trust and respect my inner world of thoughts and feelings. My thoughts mostly were about finding my pony. I felt that it was only a matter of time. I was so sure of myself that I simply knew what I *knew*. Such faith made it easy for me not to allow anybody or anything to diminish my desire to win a pony. Since the *real me* was already guiding my every thought, feeling and action, I had no need to consult anyone or anything else. I was already in touch with the depth of my soul.

From as far back as I can remember, it was clear to me that trusting my own soul and following my own heart seemed *more right* than following the opinions of others. As these pages will hopefully reveal, allowing God's whispers to guide me on my unique heart-path has enabled me to find fulfillment by sharing my gifts with others.

Being your natural, self-respecting and self-trusting person of faith allows the Universe to synchronize your actions and make your dreams come true.

Chapter 11

Watercolor Wings

"Trying Softer" means trusting your inner voice to reveal your most authentic self.

The greatest blessing I received from my pony experience is how it made it impossible for me not to have faith: Faith in myself... Faith in a Higher Power... Faith in knowing that everything is connected, and faith in my soul's longing.

Faith assures us that God, the Universe, Love, and Life always have our backs. Our prayers may not always be answered in the way we would hope for or want, but I believe there is an omniscient, benevolent force behind the scenes, continually giving us what we need.

As far back as I can remember, even before winning my pony but especially after that, I felt that what mattered most in my life was for me to share whatever gifts God granted me.

The desire to help others by becoming my best version has always kept my heart open and the love flowing. More than anything else, I believe it is my open heart that has enabled me to have an abundance of health and happiness throughout my life.

It wasn't the pony, the red saddle, or meeting the beautiful Sally Starr that set the stage for me always to have the faith and courage to pursue my dreams. Those things were the wonderful results and reflections of that central gift. What I actually *won* was a beautiful and forever pair of Spiritual Wings (Metaphorical Feathers-of-Faith) that grow each time I take a leap of faith.

Flipper

The year was 1972. I was out of the military, out of college, married with a two-year-old son, and looking for a job. I wanted a position where I could make a difference in people's lives. I'd had such a magical childhood that I wanted to have a positive influence on less fortunate kids.

My search for a job where I could help special-needs kids led me to accept a position to be a special education teacher at a residential child development center. It was a place for children with multiple handicaps to live from infancy to age 18. The kids, occupying 80 beds, suffered from such disabilities as autism, blindness, brain damage, cerebral palsy, and various other birth defects, including those caused by Thalidomide. My work granted me the privilege, as well as challenge, of teaching them basic self-care skills.

The center sat off the road a good hundred yards or so. It was built of brick and shaped like a typically long ranch home of the 1950s and '60s. Though you couldn't see them from the main road, there were three old trailers parked in the back. They were used as classrooms. Everything about the place showed age and discoloration—the walls, ceilings, furniture, and tables in the dining hall. The location, most of the time, gave off the scent of sweat and urine.

When I first interviewed for the job, I followed the director through big, thick doors, apparently leading to a dormitory area. I was startled by what sounded like a high-pitched yelping. But Mr. Ludwig, the man who became my boss, seemed unmoved and unconcerned. He kept walking onward past what looked like one tiny bedroom after another, down the long, tiled hallway. We hadn't taken many steps when out of nowhere, a small, childlike figure came roaring down the hall toward us, on a skateboard. The boy appeared to be no more than 18 inches tall, possessed a normal-sized head, but instead of arms and legs, he had small, flat appendages that looked like flippers. He used them like oars to propel himself toward our feet, rather fast.

"Tom, this is Phillip. He's our goodwill ambassador." Mr. Ludwig beamed with pride as he looked down at our friend, who I learned later, preferred to be called "Flipper."

This bright-eyed little guy had a harelip and other throat and mouth conditions that impaired his speech. Listening carefully, though, I could make out most of his words. As my skateboard greeter shouted in a high-pitched tone, from his parking space by my shoes, "Hey, I'm Flipper," I began to wonder what other world I had entered.

Phillip was a Thalidomide baby. Though he was disabled and obviously disfigured, he possessed average intelligence and a sunny disposition. He had a gentle spirit and became one of the most inspirational and certainly most unforgettable people in my life. He quickly established himself as my helper and my buddy as we worked with the other children. He had a wonderful sense of humor, especially about himself. When he wasn't rolling along beside me, in which case I had to be careful not to trip over him, he liked me to carry him.

When I met 17-year-old Phillip for the first time, I was shocked. I was embarrassed and felt awkward relating to him. My attitude soon grew into amazement, however, and finally a feeling of being honored to know this superb, life-loving teenager. The other residents had their unique gifts to share, as well, and I came to respect each of them so much.

Every day I helped as many of the children as I could to learn how to feed themselves, bathe, and participate in basic therapeutic learning activities. My favorite part of each day was helping the children learn such things as self-control, how to recognize and ask for help in meeting their needs, how to dress themselves. And for the higher functioning kids, how to speak more clearly.

But honestly, given how multiply-challenged most of these children were (some even seeming almost catatonic at times) I spent most of my time changing diapers and cleaning up various kinds of messes. Unfortunately, back then, we were severely understaffed, overworked and constantly overwhelmed, to the point where our dear residents received only minimal care.

That situation always broke my heart. To the best of my ability, I did everything I could to help the staff, as well as the children. And I loved it. I truly did. And I learned more things about love and life and myself, of course, than I can put into words. But I could bring myself to last only about a year. It was challenging trying to work with so many needy kids at the same time without any set structure or adequate help. And it really got to me how few parents of these precious children ever came to visit their displaced babies.

It was one of the richest experiences of my life. I felt truly honored to work with so many special-needs children, so intimately. I respected and loved each of them very much. And I like to think I made at least a tiny difference in the quality of many of their lives.

Mr. Ludwig said I did a great job. I guess he wasn't kidding since he literally begged me not to leave. But I needed to keep growing. I needed to create new opportunities to deepen my self-knowledge and open my heart even further. I knew that my course had to continue to help others — children and parents alike — to become healthier versions of who they were born to be.

I sent my resume to the local courthouse. It felt right to me to apply to become a juvenile probation officer. And with the door-opening assistance of more than a few, perfectly timed (non)coincidences, a panel of three judges hired me right away.

Walking Softly, Carrying a Big Brush

From the beginning, I loved everything about my new position. I felt privileged to be in such a respected and important role, the responsibility of which often felt quite daunting. The people I worked with were all amazing, talented and caring. The judges in our county were as compassionate as they were brilliant. I had high hopes, and at least a fair amount of confidence, that my counseling was going to make a difference in the lives of many troubled families. I've always loved and respected people from all walks of life.

My favorite thing about being a probation officer was being a part of a special Family Therapy unit. Remember the story about the father trying so desperately to get his frail daughter to eat? But I enjoyed every aspect of my new role. It helped that my fellow probation officers were an inspiring group of intelligent and caring individuals. My immediate supervisor Jack became my favorite person to work with.

Jack was a few years older than I. He had already been in the criminal justice field for many years. He was quite effective at handling a large caseload of delinquent youths, while simultaneously supervising a team of six probation officers. He was the go-to guy for any problem any of us had.

Though I don't think he ever purposely tried to teach me anything about counseling, I learned much from observing Jack interact with people from all walks of life. He was always respectful with everybody and a very insightful and effective counselor. Jack and I became great friends. We worked hard in our professional roles and also socialized with our families outside of the courthouse. As hard as we worked, I can't remember a day when we didn't share at least a few world-class belly laughs.

Along my path to finding my next "pony," I figured it would be a career in counseling. I couldn't imagine what else it could be. I enjoyed being a family therapist so much, I planned on creating a path toward my Ph.D. I even got accepted into a good doctoral program. I was about to discover that the Universe, God, Love, Spirit, and Life had a slightly different plan for me.

Jack's Greatest Love

Jack and I had worked together, even shared the same office, for over a year when one day I found out something quite interesting about him. This fact was something he had never even mentioned to me. One of our office secretaries told me that Jack was a wonderful artist. When I asked him about it, he shyly admitted that painting was his first love. I was surprised.

"I didn't mean to hide the fact from you, or anybody," Jack said. "It's just that for me painting is a totally spiritual and private thing. I just don't like talking about it. But yeah, it keeps me sane."

I soon learned that though he didn't talk about it, practically every doctor and lawyer in town had one of his beautiful watercolors hanging in their office or home.

Art, in general, had always interested me. In school, for example, I was always making silly doodles to make my friends laugh. Not good drawings, but just stupid creative scribbles. Other than that, however, and aside from those early paint-by-numbers horse images I had done as a kid for my room back in Oxford, I had never thought anything about painting. In fact, up until this revelation about Jack, I was one of those people who could walk into a room with beautiful paintings on the wall and hardly notice them.

Yet the moment I found out that Jack painted, something indescribable began to stir within me. I couldn't exactly identify what I was feeling, or why it mattered. But I knew to trust whatever was going on inside of me. Feeling a strong desire to see his work, I hinted to Jack to invite me to his house. He smiled and said he had been meaning to do just that. His wife had told him for months they ought to have me over.

Jack, his wife, and their son lived in a small, quaint river town called Marietta. It was a nice fall evening when I pulled up in front of their beautiful 19th Century home. I'd heard all about the work he had put into remodeling his home. I was impressed. It was beautifully restored. As soon as I walked in the front door, something pulled me like a magnet into a little room off to my left. Noticing my interest, Jack modestly said, "I guess you can call this my gallery." As his wife took my jacket, he invited me to look around. I was immediately mesmerized. I couldn't believe my eyes. The white walls of the sparsely furnished room were covered with his watercolor paintings. I was utterly overwhelmed by how beautiful they were.

Stunned, I gazed at painting after exquisite painting. These were watercolors that even an untrained eye could tell were superior, even great. They showed color in a spontaneous, vibrant richness and reflected incredible depth of feeling. The most common subjects were winter landscapes, featuring scenes of old houses and barns set against snow-covered fields.

His work showed that Jack was indeed a master artist. I was profoundly impressed by the beauty hanging on the walls of his gallery, certainly, but even more by what was going on deep inside me. I was flooded with feelings and forces that qualified as the most powerful I'd ever known.

The best way I can think of to convey the power of that moment is to compare it to the time, in 1963, when I was in the 11th grade. I sat at my desk when suddenly our grief-stricken principal reported over the loudspeaker that President John F. Kennedy had just been shot. Looking at those paintings, I was as stunned in this instance as I had been back then. In both cases, time stood still while impressions were branded in my soul.

In this situation, however, instead of shock and sadness, the opposite occurred. I was overwhelmed with positive, seemingly divine, energy and feeling a complete revelation of my own creative potential. It was like emerging from a cave after years of darkness. The light of his paintings merged with the light of my spirit. I knew at that moment, and beyond all doubt, that I too *had it in me* to express my full and loving self through painting! Everywhere I looked (and I mean everywhere, not just at those paintings) I could see only love.

But how could this be? How could I possibly know such a thing? And also, how could I not have known this about myself? Was this an epiphany? Enlightenment? Insanity?

But I didn't feel crazy. On the contrary, I felt as though the Light of my Soul was flowing generously through my heart and into every part of my being. My inner wisdom revealed to me what I had come to the Earth School to do. Now I understood that there would be more than one "pony" in my life, more than one chance to be "lucky." I could suddenly see myself helping others by bringing beautiful paintings into the world. I had felt this soulful clarity before, that intuitive voice that often contradicts what seems more rational. I'd felt it as a little boy in a small Pennsylvania town, seen it in my mother's tears and my parents' swelling pride on stage at the TV station, and happily lived with it branded in my heart ever since. I had learned what being open, unblocked and *knowing my deepest self* felt like. Now, suddenly, I faced the next revelation of who I was born to be: First and foremost, a lover of horses. We all know that. But now, somehow, and for whatever purpose the Universe has in store for me, I'd just discovered the next, deeper version of my authentic self: I was born to become an artist!

But wait! Hold your horses! I knew nada and Jack-squat about painting! I had never even thought about it. I didn't even know that watercolors came in tubes!

At first, I was so afraid to admit this epiphany to anyone, especially Jack. For months I just kept it to myself. But it was pretty much all I thought about. How could I tell Jack? What right did I have for any reason to think that I could just pick up some painting supplies and start producing exquisite watercolors, just like him? He'd already been painting for almost 20 years!

Still, on the inside, visions I couldn't deny kept coming to me, and I could *see* myself producing paintings on a level close to Jack's. As clearly as I had known as a little boy that I was destined to find my pony, I knew that I would one day be a successful watercolor artist.

Looking back on what was for me, then, the beginning of an existential identity crisis of grand proportions, I had two choices:

I could try hard to deny these "crazy impulses" and just stay safely on my path as a therapist.

I could "Try Softer" and face the truth within my heart and soul, the way I did as a boy.

I chose the latter path. My last book, *MEMO From Your Soul*, describes my transition and transformation from counselor to artist. In the chapters that follow, without rewriting that book, I'll share with you the general pathway to my becoming an artist, and where that led me. You might not be surprised to learn that another "pony" waited patiently for me.

Each time I followed my heart and launched myself off the cliff, my spiritual wings grew stronger. This time, with this artist-within transformation happening (or, I should say, for it to happen) I really needed some strong Feathers of Faith. I needed Watercolor Wings as grand as the plumage of a Philadelphia Mummer.

Chapter 12

Dancing with the Diversity of Self

"Trying Softer" means allowing yourself to pursue your purpose.

Did you ever play the game Pic-up-Stix? Remember how challenging it was to try and remove one stick at a time from the pile of scattered and intermingled sticks, looking like a pile of large, colorful toothpicks? How's that for an image and example of where, to be successful, you must try softly? Well, that's how I felt about my new, unexpected awareness that, along with being a husband, a father, a counselor, a horse lover, and a karate instructor, the real me was also born to be a watercolor artist! Wow.

This new and somehow more authentic identity was so intertwined with the rest of my life that there was no way I could reach down and simply grasp my emerging self without disturbing and moving the other sticks — ideas, beliefs, habits, fears, commitments and other patterns of behavior that had piled up over a lifetime.

Yet, at the same time, I knew I would find a way to win this new prize. The message inside me was the clearest sounding music since wanting Lucky. In my situation, however, I preferred to be prudent. After all, I was enjoying my probation job and learning from my role as a family therapist. Also, and no slight matter when others are involved (my wife and son) I was making a comfortable living with reasonable job security. A radical move would affect my family. So I made what I thought was a prudent decision: to keep the proverbial lid on this revelation until I could better understand the implications.

I also worried, at the deepest level, that somehow if I left counseling for art I would betray that essential part and purpose of who I understood myself to be. In fact, it took almost two more years before I fully accepted my need and desire to "try softly" enough to become the artist my heart was telling me I could be.

One day I got up the nerve to ask Jack if he would give me an art lesson. By then he knew enough about my dilemma to reply without hesitation, "I'll be glad to have you as my one and only private student." I couldn't hold back my tears.

"We're gonna have to start at square one," I lamented out loud. "I didn't even know that watercolors come in tubes until you told me. I can't draw very well, and I haven't held a brush since I was about eight!"

"That's all good," said Jack. "You're coming to me with no bad habits."

From then on, Jack and I talked about painting all the time. He gave me two art "lessons." I put the word lessons in quotes because all they really were was me watching Jack create one painting. As I watched him paint a beautiful landscape, featuring an old barn, I absorbed every move he made. With total concentration, I noticed every choice he made to mix colors or switch brushes. It was as if by osmosis that Jack transferred his skill and knowledge to me. The only thing he didn't have to transfer to me was his love of watercolors. That was already fully circulating throughout my being.

After those two lessons, I was off and running! I converted a tiny storage room on the side of the house we were renting into my "studio." I bought a bunch of supplies and began painting every night. As you can imagine, my first attempts were pretty feeble. I had to swallow a lot of pride (as "Trying Softer" often requires) just to dare and show Jack my childlike beginning paintings. Thankfully, he was always respectful and encouraging.

While I was trying to teach myself how to paint, I continued working in the Probation Department. I stayed in that job for three more years — three more years of intense introspection and soul-searching.

Sadly, it was during this period when Barb and I began to grow apart. By 1981, at age 35 and after seven years on the job, I realized I was fighting a losing battle within myself. The artist part of my soul was going to kick the stall door down. I knew it.

My marriage was dissolving. And not by coincidence, obviously, as I had entered this metamorphic process of turning myself (and my life) inside-out. I felt as if I was disintegrating within myself and experiencing a crisis of identity, soul deep. In such a tailspin, I was in no condition to be a partner, even to myself. I remember constantly praying with all my heart that the Universe would help me find myself again. Even the thought, not to mention the reality, was devastating: that my behavior — confusion, depression, preoccupation, worry, and obsession — was hurting my loved ones. I always tried my best to be kind and considerate, and no ounce of love in my heart was ever withheld from my son or my wife. By then I also had a beautiful little girl, Amanda.

I tried to hold on to the trying too hard way, which was to deny my own truth, but, of course, I eventually had to surrender to my inner truth, inner knowing and inner strength.

After doing our very best to keep our marriage intact, Barb and I finally agreed, for the kids' sakes as well as our own, that we would part on mutually agreed upon grounds and terms. We did so by agreement, and we even used the same attorney. We understood that we were changing only our marital status. We would always be the parents of our two beautiful children. Nothing could or would ever change or even taint that sacred blessing. She moved on as a wonderful single parent. Before long, she met a good man, who became her future husband.

I not only went off the cliff by leaving the marriage, but a few months after that, I left my probation job as well. It took every ounce of faith in me to let go of such a secure job. But I knew if I was going to bring my truest artist-self to life, I had to be one hundred percent committed to going over the edge of the cliff. It was a dive I knew I had to take to become the next best version of me.

Unlike the Japanese boy who had the goal of earning the title of Finest Karateka in all the land, my ambition was simply to become myself, day-by-day. I knew I had to keep both eyes on my path, and always in the present moment, wherever it may lead. As hard as that was to do, I realize now, looking back, that I had actually taken the "softest" path. That's because it was the path of least resistance. It was the only path I couldn't fight against.

If I was going to become an artist, just like I was going to win my pony, I had to eat, breathe and sleep that truth. To do anything less would have felt like putting my soul in a vice. Though I was scared much of the time and would be in for quite a starving artist's journey, my heart was freed to love my children even more than ever. And, of course, I was always kind, loving and respectful of their mom. Thankfully, to Barb's great credit, and our kids' great benefit, she was an absolutely wonderful mother. I helped every way I could and saw my kids regularly. Neither of us ever used our children as pawns to battle each other. We became good co-parenting partners.

At this point in my journey, I (literally, on many days) actually did become a "starving artist." I came to fully understand, in every painful way, what the phrase "Dark night of the soul" means. The only reason I was never completely homeless was because I had so many dear friends. My total annual income for my first year of earning a living painting was less than $3000.00. But I just kept painting—*persistence... persistence... persistence*—and I kept becoming more and more aligned with my truest self. I was every bit as committed to learning how to paint as I had been, as a child, trusting that my pony and I would find each other. I trusted that the best teacher I could have was the artist already living within me.

I was also deeply involved in karate during these years. That commitment and growth process helped greatly to keep my spirits up enough to fend off serious depression.

In time, my art work actually began to resemble *real* paintings. I started getting compliments from everybody. I even sold one now and then. Loving friends came to my aid time after time, to buy a painting, give me a meal, or give me a ride somewhere when my car was out of commission. Some were even so kind as to help with rent money, art supplies or framing. I felt supported by many. My buddy Ken even let me stay at his house during a period when I would have been homeless. How blessed I was, and am.

Eventually, my painting improved to the point where I was able to participate in local outdoor art shows. I regularly showed them to Jack. His feedback was consistently helpful. He always emphasized the positive things he liked about my work.

In time, I began to make enough money to support myself. I started to see that I was on the right road to making it on my own as an artist. The faith and self-confidence I relied upon, even when fear and self-doubt all but consumed me, started to pay off. I could tell that this next "pony" — becoming a successful artist — was going to happen.

One day, thanks to an amazing series of (non) coincidences, I was accepted into a top-quality art gallery outside of Philadelphia. To this day, the Chadds Ford Gallery has a world-class reputation. And just to be ironic, the gallery happened to be located only a few miles down the road from where I had kept my little Shetland, Lucky!

This was a major turning point on my beginning art path. It was an honor to be a part of such a high-level art community. It was just the boost I needed to inspire myself to keep on painting. And just the validation and inspiration I needed to keep myself open and unblocked.

Not long after I was accepted into the Chadds Ford Gallery, I learned that Jack had cancer. By that time, Jack was in his second marriage. His new partner, Linda, was his perfect soulmate. Six months later, he was gone.

My dear friend, my buddy, my boss and mentor — the angel on earth who gave me the key to unlocking the artist within — was only 53 when he took his final breath.

Before I learned of Jack's diagnosis, I had been visiting him and Linda pretty much on a monthly basis. I enjoyed taking my latest paintings to his house for critique. He was so kind and helpful. And he never hesitated to let me know how proud he was of me. I was his only "student."

Once I learned that he was ill, I visited more often. We always had wonderful conversations. There was such love and respect between us. And always laughter. Painting was such a private thing to Jack, I always felt honored that he shared everything about it with me. Next to Linda, I was the only one privileged to enter his studio. Before he died, he made sure that I would inherit all of his paints and brushes. He also instructed her to make sure I got any paintings of his that I wanted. Unfortunately, for several years leading up to the time of his passing, Jack and his only child Matt had not seen much of each other. The boy was living with Jack's ex-wife in another state. Even though they didn't spend a lot of time together, I know that Matt was Jack's pride and joy.

By this time, the choice at the fork in the road had been made. It was a done deal. No matter what, I was determined to follow the path of the artist within. I was going to allow the counselor part of me to take a back seat. Where this path would take me, I had no idea.

Who would have ever thought it would lead me to *The Lady with the Yellow Sweater?*

Chapter 13

Shock and All

"Trying Softer" means trusting the Universe to be your booking agent.

One day I received a phone call from a woman in Delaware. At the time I was living alone in an apartment in York, Pennsylvania. Even though my paintings were getting better and I was selling one now and then, I still struggled to make ends meet. It seemed that every couple of months, the electric company threatened to cut off service. If you call "living hand to mouth, but somehow managing to keep the lights and heat on most of the time" being a successful artist, then I guess I was. But it was very difficult. At the time of the phone call, I was beginning to feel depressed. When I look back on it, I think I was running out of hope. And my car would start only sometimes. You get the picture.

The reason the woman was calling was to invite me to participate in a big outdoor art show at a museum in Wilmington, Delaware. She said she had seen my work and considered it to be of the caliber the show organizers were looking for. She apologized for giving me such short notice. She said she hadn't known about me until recently.

After talking with her for a few minutes, I accepted the invitation. Hanging up the phone, I took a big gulp. What did I just do? Oh My God! I just said "yes" to doing some kind of big show, without any idea of what I will paint! I don't know what sizes to do, or how to price them, or get them framed!! Jeez-Loueeze!

My main concern was how I was going to afford enough supplies to do all of the paintings I would need. The lady had suggested at least a dozen paintings. Not to mention framing them! Oh my gosh! Along with all of those real concerns, given my car situation at the time, I couldn't even count on having transportation to get to the show. But I was already off the cliff! All I could do was pray those Mummer's wings would hold up.

I did everything I could think of to motivate myself. I prayed, I recited affirmations, I sought reassurance from everybody I knew. I even hung motivational signs on my walls. I understood this phone call, this invitation, was nothing less than a God-Send.

The show was scheduled for a Saturday in August. We ("Artists") had been assured there would be lots of pre-publicity. The organizers were expecting a huge crowd. Knowing the Brandywine Valley is a pretty wealthy area, I was very excited! I fully dedicated myself to getting ready for this show. I intended to do better work, challenging myself yet again. I borrowed a camera and a car and drove to the museum for reconnaissance. I took reference pictures of the buildings and stunning scenes along the Brandywine River. I needed photos of everything for reference, as my style is fairly representational.

The new subjects brought new energy and a chance to work on larger pieces of paper. I felt the same surging passion and determination that I had felt back in my bedroom, as a little boy determined to create the winning cattlebrand. Only this time, instead of accomplishing it in a matter of a couple of hours, I painted day and night for three months.

My friends and family all helped make this show a possibility for me. I couldn't have done it otherwise. The kind people at the local frame shop practically gave me frames. They couldn't have been more supportive. Except for a few nagging moments of self-doubt, I kept myself focused on the huge task at hand, sometimes even to the point of forgetting to eat.

Two days before the show, I received discouraging news. One of the coordinators called to tell me they expected it to rain on Saturday. She asked if I could come on Sunday instead. I told her that would be fine. As soon as I hung up, a worrisome voice in my head challenged. "What if nobody comes on the rain date?"

Sunday arrived a beautiful day. A dear friend had loaned me his van. I happily recruited my 11-year-old daughter Amanda and her friend Carole to be my helpers. I looked forward to spending the day with them.

We headed for Delaware. When we pulled into the parking lot, the attendant told us we could choose any location on the property. Expecting a hot day, we staked out our claim halfway between the cool running water of the river and the main walking path. No doubt all the paths would soon be teeming with guests. I knew I was in the right place.

As the girls and I put up my display, I lamented how unprofessional my borrowed, wood-and-chicken-wire racks looked compared to those fine aluminum frame display systems used by the other artists. But at least mine were sturdy. Plus my paintings would cover them up. I had brought 18 paintings, some of the biggest ones I ever did. They were well-framed. Overall, I was very proud and pleased by my whole display. Just being there seemed like a surreal dream come true. I was so happy to have the honor of being one among many real *artists*.

"Well, girls," I said, "its 9:30 and the gates are officially open. Bring on the customers, right?" We were ready to sell some paintings!

But what customers? There weren't any. Even by noon, the only people on the beautiful museum grounds were the artists. It was obvious that changing the date at the last minute had affected attendance. I found it very challenging to keep a positive attitude. I had worked harder than anybody would believe to get ready for this show. I had placed everything on the line. I had gone into debt and was there in a borrowed van. How was I going to keep my hopes alive now?

I had done all I could to get here, so now all I could do was relax and try, as softly as possible, to allow life to flow. I knew it was going to be a long, hot day.

The truth that kept plaguing my mind was how desperately I needed money. I didn't even have cash enough to buy the girls dinner on the way home. As the hours passed, it became painfully obvious that I was at a "no show" art show.

My fellow artists, spread throughout the many perfectly manicured acres of the park, seemed to feel the same way. They were equally disappointed and confused. It was such a beautiful day and setting. And there were so many talented artists, featuring an impressive variety of painting mediums and styles. It just didn't make any sense. The other artists counseled me, being the new kid on the block, that I might as well learn that doing art shows, indoor or out, means accepting there will be days when you sell nothing.

"We are not in this business for the money," one straw-hatted older gentleman counseled me. "We paint because it's what we love." Easy for him to say. He was comfortably retired.

Somehow, I kept the faith in spite of the lack of evidence. As I always do, I just kept saying to myself, "Well, God, it's up to you. However you want this day to go, I am thankful for your blessings." I wasn't going to allow anybody or any circumstances to diminish my faith in myself. I knew that I had been divinely guided to this place on this day.

By mid-afternoon, a few non-artists could be seen wandering along the grounds. Then I noticed two couples strolling toward my display. I had folding chairs for myself and each of the girls. Those young gals were wonderful, by the way, very patient and understanding. Here we go! I thought. Maybe one of them will buy one of my smaller watercolors. Then I could at least get my little helpers something to eat. I felt a glimmer of excitement.

Then my anxiety prompted me that maybe I should reduce my prices? I had taken a leap of faith and priced them higher than ever before, following everybody's advice that I tended to underprice my artwork.

By the time I calmed down, both couples had walked on by, chatting quietly and barely glancing at my paintings. After they had passed, one guy turned slightly, smiled, and gave me the thumbs-up sign.

The girls then asked if they should use Windex on my paintings, on the glass of the frames. "Thanks," I said. I knew they were trying their best to console me. "We might as well clean 'em before we pack them up," I said, unable to hide my disappointment.

While they were cleaning the glass, I decided to take one last walk around and visit my fellow artists. I wanted to make it a point to study their different styles. I figured at least that could be something of value I would get out of this disastrous day. We all were in sight of each other but still far apart. Walking paths provided easy access.

As I meandered around, meeting other artists and admiring their work, I realized two things: One—that I couldn't have made a mistake by being here. No matter what the outcome, there just had to be a reason for my being at this show!

Two—it was a valuable experience for me even to meet these other professional artists. Most of them were exactly what I aspired to be: full-time painters, making a living doing what they loved. Maybe that was the real point of this experience. Perhaps that was today's gift.

I opened my heart even more. I let go of all ego concerns. After all, I couldn't force the day to go any differently. I called upon all of the lessons I had learned in finding my pony. I knew God was still on my side.

By this time, it was late afternoon. Five o'clock closing time was fast approaching. The place was still a ghost town. But I had accepted things for how they were.

Admittedly still feeling a little disheartened, I walked back to my display area. I was so appreciative of the girls. All day, they had been so mature and helpful, even consoling. I intended to tell them just that.

Suddenly, Amanda came rushing up to meet me. Her face was all aglow! "Dad! Dad!" she said excitedly. "A man was just here. And a lady with a yellow sweater on. They looked rich! They asked where you were. I told them you'd be back soon. I think they really liked your paintings!"

The next thing I knew, as I stood facing my display with my back to the walking path, I suddenly heard a man's voice speak to me from behind. "Are you the artist?"

As I slowly turned, the first thing I saw was the yellow sleeve of a sweater. It was worn by an attractive older woman. She was accompanied by a very distinguished-looking gentleman.

"I want to buy some of these paintings," an authoritative voice declared.

Some? Did he say what I think he said? Some?

I stood speechless. His arm started moving. Slowly and deliberately, one at a time, he pointed to almost every painting I had on my racks. He never asked about price. He just kept saying: "I want that one…and that one… and that one." I went into shock.

In less than a minute, he bought 14 of my largest paintings! They were in the [image] size range of 22" x 30". I also had a few miniature paintings on display too, but he preferred the bigger ones.

Noticing that I was in shock, the calm, impressive man asked, "Shouldn't you be writing this down?" I scrambled for a piece of paper.

My "Fairy God-Father" didn't turn out to be just the president of a large credit card bank. *Of course*, he was a world-class art collector, as well!

By trying hard enough, but not too hard — keeping faith in myself, and in God, the Universe, Love and Life — I had just won another "pony"!

By the time the art show was over, in addition to selling 14 paintings to the bank president, I also sold one small painting to another artist. That kind lady paid cash, so the girls and I had more than enough money for dinner.

At the end of the day, I had a smile on my face, a glow in my heart, a fire in my soul and a check in my hand for over five-thousand dollars! Plus I had an appointment scheduled for me to meet my new patron. I was invited to the bank's headquarters in Wilmington, the following week!

At my meeting with the bank president, I happily signed a contract agreeing that I would paint at least three paintings a month, for the bank, for the next two years. The contract stated that as long as both parties were happy with the commissioned work, the option would remain open for us to continue the arrangement. Indefinitely.

And that is what happened. For the next 15 years, I painted an average of three paintings a month. I painted them knowing they were sold even before I signed them. The agreement allowed me to price them however I thought was fair. I was careful to err on the side of not overpricing them. I couldn't be anything but fair and generous to such a God-sent benefactor. My original watercolors were used to decorate the halls and offices of the many facilities the bank owned, worldwide.

Concerning "Trying Softer," just as I had whole-heartedly believed in myself to win the pony from Sally Starr, once again, I had proof that: Trusting yourself and your connection with God, the Universe, Love and Life is the path of optimum manifestation.

As by now, you probably expect me to say: This *serendipitous* encounter between the bank president and me had nothing to do with luck. Instead, it took blood, sweat, and tears, complete faith in myself and my connection to all of life, and a fair amount of courage, for me to allow myself to be at that fateful art show on that precise day.

At the heart of "Trying Softer" is the understanding that we are all guided by whispers from God.

Every day, you have choices. You have a choice to accept, block or over-ride the divine messages from within. Such whispers from your heart come courtesy of your conscience and most profound intuition. If you try too hard to second-guess yourself and allow fear to steer you off course, you may never meet your angel — in any colored sweater.

I call this chapter "Shock and All" because, on that amazing day at the outdoor art show, I actually did go into shock when I heard that voice saying, "I want to buy some of these paintings." *It shocked me* to be struck, for the second time, by a bolt of *LIGHTNING*, as I was by the T-Horseshoe cattle brand!

The "All" in my chapter title means that once the artist in me was so completely validated, that was "All" I needed to navigate the rest of my life-journey.

In her acclaimed book, "Return to Love" (Harper Collins, 1992) Marianne Williamson reminds us: "Our deepest fear is not that we are inadequate. Our deepest fear is that we are powerful beyond measure. It is our light, not our darkness that most frightens us. We ask ourselves, who am I to be brilliant, gorgeous, talented, and fabulous?

"Actually, who are you not to be? You are a child of God. Your playing small does not serve the world. There is nothing enlightened about shrinking so that other people won't feel insecure around you. We are all meant to shine, as children do. We were born to make manifest the glory of God that is within us. It is not just in some of us; it is in everyone. And as we let our own light shine, we unconsciously give other people permission to do the same. As we are liberated from our own fear, our presence automatically liberates others."

Chapter 14

Two Hearts are Better Than One

"Trying Softer" means believing in miracles.

At that blessed and amazingly synchronistic art show in 1989, my dream to make a living through my painting came true. The banker ended up hiring me to paint regularly, to add to his world-class art collection. He wanted original paintings to fill the hallways and offices of all of the bank's buildings. Because he had facilities around the world, there was no shortage of wall space. Though a pale comparison, my arrangement with the banker was so mutually beneficial that it often reminded me of the classic relationship between the wealthy Medici family (13th century Italy) and struggling artists of that era, most notably, Michelangelo.

While not a single cell of my brain can fathom, even as a joke, any comparison between me and such a genius of the Renaissance, of course, I did feel the soulful kind of gratitude I'm sure any artist would feel when having a wealthy and fully supportive patron. It was the same soulful validation I'd felt getting my pony on Sally Starr's show. Because I had

"Tried Softer," stayed open and true to myself and the inner whispers of God through my heart, I was able to connect with the perfect person—the man who wanted, needed and could afford my art the most.

One night at the banker's home we were first discussing my painting contract. I thought I was hearing things when he turned to me and said: "You can determine your own salary, Tommy."

"What?" How many employees get to hear their bosses make such a statement?

I felt honored that he trusted me to price my paintings at fair market value. Which I did, of course, taking everything into account, including that he was buying so many. To err on the side of not taking advantage of this great man and this extraordinary opportunity, I priced each painting on the low side. Occasionally, to show my appreciation for the opportunity I had, I even donated paintings to the bank.

My wonderful banker friend—husband of the lady in the yellow sweater—was indeed a very kind man with a huge heart.

Soon after I signed my contract with the bank, I moved in with Rose. She was beautiful, caring and kind. At the beginning of the relationship, we complemented each other well. I was the absent-minded, disorganized artist, and she did a great job of handling the business side of my career.

One of the many ways Rose showed me love and support was by helping me renovate her old springhouse into the perfect little studio for me. I'll always be grateful to her for that kindness. You can see it if you go to my website and check out my watercolor demonstrations on Youtube: www.sageandbrush.com

For the first year or so, the banker told me what he wanted me to paint. Typically, that meant portraits of the bank's buildings, flower gardens around the property or other scenes related to bank functions. A typical example would be painting scenes of jugglers and other entertainment activities at their "Corn boil," the bank's annual summer picnic. Soon I was granted the freedom to paint whatever inspired me. That's when I added lighthouses, landscapes, flowers, and marine scenes—all kinds of subjects.

I was living (and loving) my dream of painting for a living. At the end of each month, when I had a batch of paintings finished, all I needed to do was deliver the unframed paintings to the bank and pick up a check. How could an artist have a better arrangement?

At the same time, I felt the truth of that classic adage of "Be careful what you wish for." I was only one person—one artist—learning on the job. As committed as I was (and believe me, my soul was on fire to please my Fairy God-father by making each painting better than the last), I really had to struggle at times to keep up the pace. Often the banker wanted even more paintings than I could turn out! And he almost always wanted them sooner than I could produce them. I did my best, of course, to accommodate his deadlines, but never at the expense of quality. He understood and respected that about me. I got it—and I loved it—that his bottom-line motivation for hiring me was to help me realize my fullest potential as a human being, not just as an artist.

Working for the bank was one of the greatest blessings of my life. It was a God-sent opportunity that helped me in every way. I learned a lot about painting... I got to travel a little... I got to teach watercolor painting to disadvantaged students at a private Catholic school... I got to meet all kinds of interesting people and make many new friends... I was able to have a steady income for the duration of my contracts with the bank... and, most of all, I grew as a person.

After all I had been through to finally get to that place of being an artist—all the risking, struggle and transitions of faith, trusting God and the Universe, as I did when I was a mere child searching for my pony—can you imagine how blessed I felt? What an incredible situation to be in. Most surprising to myself was to be able to paint what I wanted, how I wanted, all the while knowing each painting was sold before I even put brush to paper! I was in heaven most of the time I worked for the bank.

As a mentor, the banker taught me many things about myself, including that I was capable of producing works of art beyond what I could have imagined. It was like being in the ultimate Art School. He was the teacher, every day inspiring me to release all blocks to my artist potential, while I was getting paid to do what I loved! Not a bad gig. Obviously, that "feeling" I had in Jack's house, back in the days of working in the probation office, was indeed a whisper from God about what path I should take. What if I had not listened to that message? What if I had squelched it, because of fear? Thank God, I took the "Try Softer" path of acceptance, rather than the hard path of denying my true identity.

I always knew my dream job would not last forever. Sure enough, 15 years after I first saw that yellow sweater, one day the banker suddenly retired. Botta boom!!! No ifs, ands, or buts, that was it. I was instantly unemployed!

The situation was more complicated than I'm going to describe here, but suffice it to say it was not an easy adjustment for Rose or me. It definitely put a strain on our already suffering relationship.

Basically, what happened was this: When I first learned that my dream job had ended, I went into shock, just as I had back when I first met the banker at that fateful art show. While that shock was linked with joy, this shock was caused by fear, sadness, and disappointment. I can't say I was devastated or even totally surprised because I'd always known that this day would come. But it was so crazy sudden! That's what threw me the most. I'd been so totally mind/body/spirit invested in painting for the banker and the bank that I really wasn't prepared for the assignment to be over.

Though I was thrown for a giant loop, I knew enough about myself to stay open and accept everything I was feeling. This included the anger I felt, as well as the guilt for being angry.

All the while I felt mad and somehow betrayed, I wondered how could I possibly think anything negative about the banker or the bank? They had done nothing but bless me. What kind of crazy entitlements did I feel? But I went easy on myself. I knew it was all about fear, and perfectly natural, given my level of commitment. It was as powerful as any divorce. One minute I was dedicated to my painting mission, mind/body/soul. The next thing I knew, I was told I would be separating from all the things and people I had loved for 15 years, including the regular painting (and income).

It took me several months to get my new bearings. During that time, especially given that my relationship with Rose was on a downward spiral, I came close to feeling some serious depression. But, thankfully, with a healthy measure of self-acceptance and the support of family and friends, I soon began to see the new opportunity I faced.

It was clear that I stood at a critical fork in the road. One path, the "Try Harder" path, would have meant getting angry, feeling sorry for myself, thinking the Universe let me down, developing a sour attitude and, probably, eventually getting sick. The other path, the "Try Softer" path, which, of course, is the one I took, gave me the opportunity to get to know, honor and share more of myself. That path meant taking advantage of the opportunity the Universe had just given me to slow down, take a breath and relax into some very deep soul searching.

That's when I decided I needed to write a book about my harmonious dance with the Universe. I felt the desire to write a book explaining that my good fortune was not simply "luck." I knew it was my belief in myself and my unshakeable faith that enabled me to find my pony, at age 10, and then three decades later—in the right place at the right time—meet my dream-maker banker, teacher, and friend. I knew that writing such a book would be a valuable, cathartic exercise to put my life in perspective. My primary purpose was rooted in my soul's mission to help other people see the benefits of trusting themselves.

So one day, I pulled out an old Royal typewriter and began writing *Memo From Your Soul*. I had no idea where to begin or how even to write a legitimate paragraph. But again, relying on the same faith that had brought me both my pony and my painting livelihood, I trusted that if I didn't create blocks within myself, the words would flow from my heart. And that's what happened.

The process of writing *MEMO* took about three years. It was three years of learning everything I needed to learn— from how to use a computer, to finding an agent, to finding a publisher. Phew-w-ww! Thank God I tried hard enough, but not too hard. Eventually, and joyfully, I ended up with a book that I had both written and illustrated!

A Heaven-sent Heart

During that period of writing my book, I had begun counseling others as a life coach. Helping others helped me feel better about myself. I felt that my clients truly appreciated the real me, more than my partner did. That may not have been true, but that is how I felt at the time. Looking back, I can see how I desperately needed real intimacy in my relationships, based on authenticity and non-judgment, much more profound than just surface communication. And actually, I became a pretty effective counselor. I helped several clients, from various states, through phone consultation, to remove blocks to their happiness.

When it came to seeing how others needed to incorporate change into their own lives, I found that was easy. When it came to me fully admitting the depth of my own pain, at the time, I blocked myself. I just could not admit how hurt and sick I felt deep down in a relationship that wasn't soul-satisfying.

I must admit, I debated whether to share the following story with you, only because it is so unbelievable. But everything I'm going to describe is true:

I'll always remember the day my published books, hot off the press, were delivered to my house. I opened the front door in record time. I hurried onto the front porch, picked up the box and brought it into the house. I sat in my favorite chair and tore off the strapping tape. I opened the box.

Wow. I can still remember the smell. And what a beautiful sight! There they were — a stack of 25 new books (MY OWN!) It was such a thrill to see and touch them. I picked out a fresh copy of my book. It was an unforgettable moment. But it was a moment I had to experience alone.

I could have called a friend and celebrated over the phone. But that wouldn't have satisfied the loneliness I felt in my heart. At that pivotal moment, especially, I wished that I had a partner who could be as happy as I was about this achievement.

Rose was home at the time, doing different chores around the house. I'm sure a part of her was happy for me. She did congratulate me. I think because her interests and priorities, at that time, were less aligned with me becoming a new author than her natural concerns about more practical matters such as the state of our relationship and our finances, etc., we were not able to have the kind of deeply appreciative, heart-to-heart moment of celebrating and sharing that I would have liked.

But that was OK, and I understood. I had no ego investment in what the book was about or why I had written it. I had written it to help people. And I was filled with the hope that it would. So even without being able to fully share the depth of the experience the way I would have preferred, after putting so much of my heart into writing the book for so many years, my soul felt indescribably satisfied to finally have my cherished memoir (*MEMO FROM YOUR SOUL*) in my hands.

I sat alone in my living room, holding my book, staring at it, and reminding myself of all the people I hoped to help.

After Rose went outside, I carried one of my new books upstairs with me. I placed it on the nightstand beside my bed. Rose and I had occupied separate bedrooms for several years. I left the room and went to another. Just two minutes later, upon returning to the bedroom, I noticed something was sitting on top of my book.

Because I was the only one upstairs, I was dumbfounded by how anything could be lying on top of the book that just a couple of minutes earlier I'd placed on the table. That was not possible!

I walked over to the book. Lying on top of my book was a beautiful heart-shaped necklace. I knew there was no way anyone could have put that there. And I knew I hadn't.

I started to weep. I understood, in ways I can't explain, that this beautiful heart necklace had manifested for me as a gift from God. It wasn't there. Then it was.

Intuitively, I felt it was a gift of love and support from my departed maternal grandmother. We had always been particularly close. She had always supported my creative side, and I always felt her love and support. Even while writing the book, over a three-year period, I'd often heard her supportive whispers in my heart.

The heart necklace was beautiful. It didn't look or feel like any ordinary piece of jewelry. The heart itself seemed to be something other than glass or plastic. It almost looked like a combination of both. Maybe with some other elements added. It was really unusual.

It has little, concentric, heart-shaped rings that are translucent and kind of pinkish-red. It is a mysterious object in every way. It has become my most precious possession. I cherish it as a reminder that our departed loved ones always look out for us.

It is precisely because this heart story is so amazing that I decided I wanted everyone to know about it. However it got there—even if Rose or somebody else snuck into the house, ran upstairs and plunked it down on my book within the two minutes I was out of the room—I still find it soulfully validating.

But Rose was working outside. Plus, I know she wouldn't have done it. She even swore it wasn't or couldn't have been her. And no one else was in our home at the time. Also, where I was when I was out of the bedroom, really for just a couple of minutes, I would have seen anyone coming upstairs. I considered my heaven-sent heart necklace to be a manifestation and a symbol proving that love is not subject to limitations or boundaries. Believe it or not!

But wait – there's more!

I immediately put my heart necklace in a place of safekeeping. Then one day, a few months later, I walked into a newly plowed field behind our house. I went there to toss out some leftover food scraps. The sun was on its way down. It was a beautiful evening. As I was about to head back to the house, I suddenly noticed something shining in the dirt. It was about 20 feet away and beautifully reflecting the sunlight. Curious, I walked over to it. When I looked down, I couldn't believe my eyes. There was (another!!) little shiny heart gleaming in the sun! This one was not filled in, like the other one. Instead, it was more like an outline of a heart, with the heart-shaped center space open. It seemed to be made of some kind of light, but naturally strong, metal. It didn't have a string or chain on it like my necklace heart. It was just a shiny little heart.

Even though it happened before, in the big and mysterious way you just read about, I was as amazed finding this heart in the middle of a plowed field as I was the book-gift from beyond. Of course, by the way, the little heart wasn't dirty at all.

Feeling blessed and somehow validated once again, I decided to keep it in my car. It's such a cool surprise, I thought. Maybe it will keep me safe in my travels. For that reason, I put it in the glasses case located on the interior roof of my car. Since it was a new car, nothing else had ever been in that compartment. I planned to keep it there and allow it to provide whatever "good mojo" it had in store for me.

A few weeks later, I decided to take my youngest grandson to a nearby park. He was about four years old. His favorite thing at the park was the tire-swing. I loved pushing him back and forth and round and round. We laughed and talked about everything under the sun. One summer, we even got to watch two baby hawks grow from hatchlings to flying adults. It was just a great place for any grandpa and his grandson to be.

On this particular occasion, as I pulled into the park, for some reason, I suddenly thought of the little glasses-box heart. And I decided to show it to my grandson. I pulled to a stop and turned off the car. "Hey, Buddy," I asked, "would you please do me a favor and put your hand up into that glasses compartment and feel around? My fingers are too big. I want to show you something I found." I was thinking I could make a fun treasure hunt game for us by maybe hiding the sparkly heart somewhere in the park.

The little boy reached up and felt all around. "I don't feel anything, Pap," he said. Then I reached up and did my own tactile search. I couldn't feel anything either. I couldn't understand. How could the compartment be empty?

I didn't say anything more about it to my grandson, other than thanking him for the effort. Inside, however, I felt confused. I even felt somehow betrayed. As ridiculous as that might sound, I couldn't help but wonder why God would give me this little field-heart and then take it away. I was mystified by the whole thing. All I could think to do was ask God to give it back to me. I had felt so blessed to have found it and instantly loved it so much.

One day, at least a month later, on the spur of the moment and after I had pretty much forgotten about the little heart, I wheeled into a convenience store to get something to drink. I pulled into a parking space, turned off the car and went into the store. When I came out and was about to slide back into the front seat, something caught my eye. I noticed a shiny little object lying directly on top of the console between the two front seats. Yep, as I'm sure you can guess, there it was! My little, shiny, gift-from-the-gods heart was positioned smack dab in the middle of the console, glimmering in the afternoon sun! It hadn't been there—and then it was.

Don't you love it when such miracles happen!

The Mysterious Universe

Whether we recognize it, acknowledge it or believe it, miracles, mysteries and all kinds of unexplained things happen all the time and all over the place. Commonly, we are afraid to share such stories because people might think we're crazy.

Oh… Here's another one! About a month ago, I was alone in my living room. I sat on the couch in front of a big wooden coffee table. The TV was off and all was quiet. I was lost in thought, looking over some of this manuscript. Suddenly, I heard a penny drop onto the coffee table in front of me. It startled me, it was so loud. It was as if a hand had just tossed it there from about six inches above the wooden surface. It made a very distinct penny-hitting-wood sound. I distinctly heard it bounce and spin. When I looked up, sure enough… there was a penny!

What can I tell you? It literally dropped out of nowhere. It hadn't been there—and then it was. I heard it land. It came from "somewhere!"

All I know is, I didn't toss it and fool myself! Amazing! We can't yet explain such manifestations. And that's OK. It's OK to simply accept that we don't have to be able to figure everything out.

I mention these true yet unbelievable events to reinforce with you that "Trying Softer" means being open to all that is. Think about all of the amazing coincidences you've had in your life. I'm sure there have been lots of synchronicities and confluences, impossible to adequately explain, beyond just announcing that they happened.

"Trying Softer" means surrendering to the fact that we don't know everything. It means accepting that being human is a flying-by-the-seat-of-our-pants, trusting-in-the-Universe proposition.

My Sally Starr pony experience taught me, at age 10, to respect all mysteries of the Universe. The pages you are heading into now offer further examples of how — when you are in spiritual alignment — the Universe will provide everything you need, even beyond Heavenly Hearts.

What else was I seeking? Even I wasn't fully aware of that one. But I knew it would mean going really deep. The challenge was going to be not to try too hard.

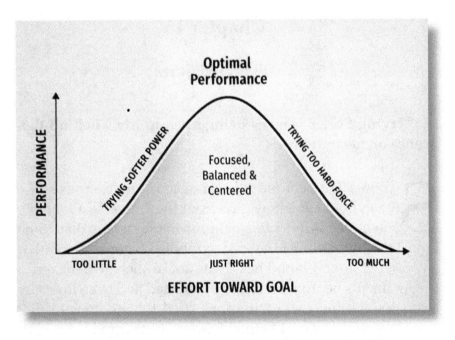

The above chart shows the importance of BALANCE. Of course, to do anything, you need to put forth some effort. Sometimes a tremendous amount. But as soon as you lose sight of the fact that you also need to remain focused, aligned, balanced, relaxed and centered in order to achieve optimal success, your actions become counterproductive.

Chapter 15

Synchrodestiny

"Trying Softer" means being open to life's behind-the-scenes orchestrations.

S o now I had a couple of *hearts*, each as mysterious as the other, both somehow gifts from the Universe, God, Life and Love. As I've said, to me, no matter where they came from, they were much-needed symbols of hope, given that my own flesh-and-blood heart was not in such great shape.

Again, it's not that I wasn't appreciated and even loved by everyone around me. I felt appreciated for the things I did, certainly all the ways I helped Rose and her family. And I'm sure they loved me and appreciated the things I did. It's just that for whatever reasons, within my marriage, I never felt soulfully supported for who I was as a person.

Though I felt guilty for even thinking it sometimes—as if something was wrong with me for not being satisfied with a sort of safe, comfortable lifestyle—I just couldn't shake the feeling—the truth—that I wanted unconditional, not conditional, love. I felt confident that I was good at giving it, but my soul was hurting. Something vital was missing in my relationship. I would soon find out what that something was.

After my long-standing painting job (opportunity of a lifetime!) ended, I stepped up my private counseling. It gave me something valuable and healing to do. It also brought in a little money. Mostly, as I knew, I wanted to help others because that practice always brought me closer to myself.

Soon I had gained four regular clients: Summer and Liz would call me every other week from Arizona. Laura would call weekly from North Carolina. And every other Wednesday, Bev would stop by the house for counseling. I could call these wonderful women "clients." But in every case, if they weren't to begin with, they all soon became dear friends. So much so that after a while, I just kept talking with them and helping them without any payment. The main reward for me was my own growth.

I felt as I had felt back in the days when I was a psychotherapist at our local mental health center. In those days, seeing eight or nine clients a day, I always believed I was the one gaining the most insight. HELPING OTHERS IS "A" IF NOT "THE" MOST EFFECTIVE WAY TO HEAL YOUR OWN HEART. And that is what I was doing. At the same time, I was trying to keep myself from really facing my own unhappy heart.

Yes, I had won a pony... yes, I had become the artist I'd dreamt about... yes, I had a good life with people who cared about me, and yes... I had good health. And the biggest Yes of all: I have the most wonderful kids and grandkids on earth. I was fully aware of all of my blessings. On the surface, it looked as though I had everything. But what I didn't have and always longed for was my true partner, my Soulmate. I wanted to be happy with a woman who loved me for who I am.

Yet I wasn't actively looking for another partner. I was only trying to help my friends find happiness in their own lives and relationships. It was in that process that I found enough intimacy to feel the kind of sustaining validation I longed for. Intimacy, of course, meant to me nothing more than honest, heart-to-heart communicating.

For whatever reasons—and I accept that it was mostly my issue—I wasn't able to meet Rose at that soulful place of honest authenticity. The level of compatibility that I needed just wasn't there. And even though I saw no signs that we could ever find that harmonious place to meet, I wasn't planning to divorce Rose. I figured I would just keep working on myself.

Though I had been trained in various counseling techniques, I knew that speaking from my heart was the most therapeutic thing I could do, for myself as well as my "clients." To help me become a more sensitive and effective counselor, I embarked on a study of something called "Heart IQ."

The founder of "Heart IQ" is Christian Pankhurst. I consider him to be the leading authority on heart-centered communication and heart-intelligent relationships. His method, which is relatively specific, is my favorite coaching framework. Speaking from the heart is something that has always come naturally to me.

For reasons you will soon understand, I need to ask you to please remember the term "Heart IQ."

The second life-coaching modality I used was based on a book by Richard Rudd called *Gene Keys*. It's an amazing book describing how each of us has a particular path in life as unique as our fingerprints. It's much more than that, though. It's a book you can study for a lifetime, jammed full of wisdom and the latest information about what it means to be human.

Please remember the term "Gene Keys" too.

I need you to remember both "Heart IQ" and "Gene Keys." These are the two specific counseling modalities I chose to embrace, out of many other approaches. Both ways, strategies or methods of getting to know your true self were wonderfully effective.

One day, another friend of mine, Bonnie, invited me to her house for dinner. Bonnie had always been as much a counselor to me as I was to her. She knew me well. She was up-to-date on everything I was involved in, including my two favorite methods of self-growth—Yep, "Heart IQ" and "Gene Keys."

"Have a seat, Tommy. I have a story to tell you." She wore a Cheshire Cat smile on her face. "I think you might find it very interesting.

"You know Bev has an art show going on downtown, right?" Bonnie asked.

"Yes," I replied. (The Bev she was referring to was one of the women I had been counseling.) "I went there with Kate last night. And while I was there, my friend Judy came in. She was with her boyfriend. I don't know if I ever told you about Judy before. But she is very spiritual. Really an incredible woman. She is one of my dearest friends in the world, next to you, of course. And she is absolutely beautiful, inside and out! Well… she and her boyfriend do drum circles. You know what those are, right? I think Chris is a great guy too. He's really quite the accomplished musician.

"Anyway, like you, Judy's always been kind of a life coach to everybody she meets. I don't know exactly what her education is, but I'm sure she's studied psychology and all forms of therapy. She's an expert in nutrition and all things healthy. She's really a cool person, very science-based, as well as metaphysical. Always interested in growth and self-improvement. You know.

"Yadda, yadda, yadda… enough about her background. When she came in the door at Bev's show, I was totally surprised. And really happy to see her. I hadn't seen her, I'll bet, in three years. When she came in, I ran over to give her a hug. I asked her how she was, and how she was doing. She said 'good.' She looked really happy and healthy. Then

I asked her—now are you paying attention, Tommy? Here comes the good part—just the general question: 'So what are you up to these days?' You know me; I have to know everything about everybody. And now… I'm just going to tell you what she said. You can do whatever you want with this information. Her exact words were: 'Aside from the drum circles, I'm doing some counseling. And I'm studying two very interesting things. They're kind of self-help modalities that you probably never heard of. They're not that well-known yet, both out of England. One is called 'Heart IQ,' and the other is really a book. It's called *Gene Keys*."

(Note to reader: Upon hearing that, I was in total disbelief. WOW!! I should probably end this book right here. You talk about coincidence! And synchronicity! Holy Cow! And then some!)

Continuing, Bonnie said: "When I heard that, my jaw hit the floor! What are the odds in a small town in rural Pennsylvania, anybody, let alone my two best friends, would be studying the exact same counseling modalities at the same time? But hey, as you know, there are no coincidences. Isn't that amazing?"

I just smiled and shook my head. "Did you tell her about me?" I asked excitedly.

"No, why should I?" Bonnie teased. "I didn't think she'd be interested." Her laugh resounded in the room. "OF COURSE, I told her about you! I told her: 'You have to meet Tom Newnam! He's studying both of those things too!'

"How'd she react to that?"

"After she almost fainted, she asked: 'Who's Tom Newnam?'"

Bonnie went on to share that she told Judy more about me, and Judy said she would love to meet me. She said she was thrilled to know that someone else was studying the big *Gene Keys* book. She'd been searching for someone else to help her explore the book but didn't think anybody in this area would know of it. Bonnie said that she gave Judy my email address.

I thanked Bonnie for bringing all of this together—however she did—and that, of course, I'd be more than happy to meet Judy.

I learned long ago that such coincidences are at the very least, valuable "signposts" that the people involved are somehow on the right track. Plus, like Judy, I was having a difficult time fathoming the depth of the *Gene Keys* book as well, so I welcomed the collaboration. I was totally open to anything that might help both Judy and me to assist our clients better. I didn't know how, what, where or when, but I knew Judy was a gift from God.

At that time, I was fairly busy with my regular clients. Additionally, I was heavily involved in doing some paintings for the Chadds Ford Gallery, so I wasn't all that concerned about whether she was going to contact me. I knew we'd meet one day. I didn't see how that couldn't happen.

Sure enough, the next day after my talk with Bonnie, I received an email from Judy. She introduced herself, talked about the "unbelievable coincidence" and asked how much I charged for counseling. She said she had a few difficulties in her personal life that she thought I could help with. I came up with a token figure and invited her to come to my studio on January 23. We were only a couple of days into January at the time, giving us both time to reschedule if something came up. Obviously, we both looked forward to meeting each other.

I wrote "Judy" on my calendar for January 23. I didn't think too much about our scheduled meeting, other than realizing the whole event as an amazing coincidence. I knew all of the things I had to experience and all the specific events that had to happen for me to discover the *Gene Keys* book. And the same with "Heart IQ"! I was astounded that anyone else would have zeroed in on those two particular self-help instruments, tools, methods, modalities. Obviously, the whole Universe was behind this one.

And what if our mutual friend Bev hadn't produced an art show? Bonnie and Judy might not have reunited.

Wow! What is it with these art shows? First, mine and the lady in the yellow sweater, and now... who knows what! I was intrigued.

Somehow, though, I kept my mind on other things and went on about my business. Judy sent me a couple of other anticipatory emails. In one, she said: "I heard you wrote a book." (That was my *MEMO From Your Soul*.) She went on to admit that she felt a little intimidated meeting a "real author." I thought that was cute, kind and refreshingly honest.

So, as I say, our meeting was arranged to happen on the 23rd. On the 16th day of that month (a week earlier), I was having a normal day. I did a little painting in the morning. After lunch, taking advantage of snow on the ground, I decided to burn some accumulated brush. The burn pile bordered the large field where I had found that little heart. You remember — the heart that disappeared from my car and then reappeared weeks later.

About 1:30 I decided that, rather than take a shower after burning stuff all morning, I wanted to go into my studio and do a little more painting, and that's what I did.

I was in the studio, looking at my painting — trying to organize my thoughts — when unexpectedly I heard "knock knock knock"!

It was obviously a feminine knock. I honestly had no clue who it could be. Generally, when I was in my studio, no one would bother me. I didn't have a sign asking for privacy, as I usually welcomed visitors. But if I had the shade on the door pulled all the way down, which it was this day, that signaled I was probably busy painting. I knew it wasn't Rose. And I didn't think it was my daughter Amanda. I was completely baffled. I walked across the floor and opened the door.

A beautiful woman stood before me. It wasn't just that her face was lit up and smiling. Her whole being seemed to glow.

Her hair, her eyes, her body—in her pretty workout clothes and sneakers—everything about her was stunning.

Even as she stepped into my studio, I had no idea who she was. Yet the expression on her face showed that I should have been expecting her.

The next thing I knew, and with no words spoken, we stood in the middle of my studio hugging each other. The feeling was as if we were long-lost friends once again united.

My mind was spinning. It was a crazy feeling because I just couldn't place this person. Of course, you know who it was. But honestly, it never occurred to me that this was Judy. I guess I had it so fixed in my mind that she was scheduled to come the following week. Finally, it hit me: This must be Judy! She had *mistakenly* come a week early. Holy Cow!

I no sooner realized who she was than I also remembered how I looked. Oh man! Thoughts tumbled in my mind. I'm totally covered in soot and grime. What will she think of me? Will she think this is how I prepare for guests? That this is my jerky idea of making a good first impression? But... wait... if I tell her she came on the wrong date, she might leave. I definitely don't want that. Yet how can I act like I was expecting her? She's already seen the stupid look on my hippie-hobo face!

All of those thoughts and a million more raced through my mind, all the while we still embraced! There was no way around it; I was simply caught in the act of being myself. I had no place to hide, and no explanation to offer.

What did I do? Once again, I pulled out the old "Surrender it all to God" card. After all, I figured, God set this whole thing up in the first place. Obviously, Judy is *supposed* to be here today.

We finally stopped hugging. Judy sat down. I sat across from her. We stared at each other. The instant kindred-spirit recognition between us was stunningly powerful. I successfully released any ego concerns about myself and focused on her. I wanted to be totally open to who and all this beautiful woman was.

We had a wonderful conversation—an easy kind of back and forth—Tell me about your life... Tell me about this and that. Every now and then, without any thought or coordination between us, we spontaneously stood up, walked toward each other, met in the middle of the room and held each other's hands. Then we would, in the same synchronized way, let go of each other's hands and sit down. We must have repeated that dance five or six times. Amazing!

During our first meeting, I don't think we even mentioned the *Gene Keys* or "Heart IQ." We were too eager to get to know each other, more than curious to find out how it could be that we were somehow, already, instant life-long friends.

Of course, Bonnie was thrilled to have connected Judy and me. She loved the story of our first encounter. Especially the part of me looking like I had just fallen off the turnip truck.

Judy and I developed an every-other-Thursday schedule for visits. We even looked at the *Gene Keys* book sometimes. Mostly, we shared our most sincere truths with each other, straight from our hearts.

We had so much in common. We were both parents and grandparents, and therapists. We were both lovers of people, growth, and all matters of higher consciousness and metaphysics. Our conversations were very rich. We quickly opened ourselves to each other. From the soul... to the heart... to our thoughts and feelings, with complete trust and authenticity, we validated each other at the deepest level.

Though there was an obvious mutual attraction, we both were in committed relationships at the time. Though mine had been unsatisfying for many years, Judy was in a very happy relationship. At the time, neither of us was even thinking about leaving our partners, or in any way having an affair. The bottom line for both of us—in our relationships with ourselves, each other and our partners—was respect.

I waited until her second visit to confess to my new friend the truth about the day she had first come to my studio. I told her that, though I knew she never realized it, she'd actually been a week early. I first gave her the noble excuse that I didn't want to embarrass her. Then I confessed that the main reason I didn't say anything about the date mix-up was because I was afraid she would have left. I further explained how ashamed and embarrassed I felt, not being cleaned up enough to present even a decent appearance. We laughed about how black my face was.

After hearing all of that—so typically Judy, so very kindly—she smiled and assured me that she hadn't even noticed. "It was your soul that greeted me, Tom. And I could see right away how pure and beautiful that is."

Wow! Who is this woman? This level of acceptance, this honoring of my soul, this level of intimacy. This was what I'd always longed for.

Apparently, this was a woman I could relate to from the deepest part of my being. It wasn't about sex, or looks, anything ego-related, or any kind of clever personality dance. It was about two authentic, heart-centered, growth-loving souls connecting naturally, and somehow (as we both intuitively knew) for the betterment of all.

Chapter 16

Tears of Recognition

"Trying Softer" means accepting that you are worthy of love.

O ne night not long after meeting Judy, I was sleeping soundly in a bedroom separate from Rose's. Around 4:00 a.m., I awakened to warm tears running down my cheeks. In spite of years of being in an unfulfilling relationship, I was surprised that I was crying. In all 67 years of my life, I couldn't remember ever crying myself awake.

Because of my background in the mental health field, I knew that crying is one of the healthiest and most healing things a person can do. In my role as a psychotherapist, I used to reassure my clients: "You should never feel ashamed of crying. It is a beautiful sign of strength and resilience. It is one of our body's most natural and effective ways of processing our deepest emotions. Like laughter, crying is a wonderful release of all those things we can't put into thoughts or words."

Though that kind of insight served me with my clients, it did little to reassure me, on this lonely night, that I was having a healthy experience. I could tell that something stirred within me, something I wasn't quite in touch with.

As I lay in bed weeping, my focus turned to discovering the cause. I wasn't sobbing, just steadily shedding tears. I reflected upon my childhood. It was barely daybreak, so I knew I had plenty of time and privacy to identify what was ailing me. Being no stranger to introspection, I figured I'd solve the mystery of the flowing tears by 7:00 or 8:00. I told myself that by that time, I'd hop out of bed, better off for the cathartic experience.

Soon it was 6:00. By then I had reviewed my entire life. But there was no sign of the tears stopping. That's when I realized that I was, or God was, unlocking all parts of myself for me to discover.

For some reason, I created an image of it as the turning of a combination lock on a safe where the real me was locked inside. Whether that was the best analogy or not, I could tell this introspective journey was going all the way to its destination. I was going to be introduced to my bottom-line, most real and authentic self, no matter where or why I was hiding... like it or not. Attempting to confine this process to my head, I theorized my way out of feeling everything. But I could tell, and it frightened me to know, that this was going to be a full-body experience.

But why now? Was I really that soulfully unhappy? I had never thought or at least admitted to myself, that I was THAT unhappy. I had been aware for a long time that I was in an unfulfilling relationship. But why, all of a sudden, such unstoppable tears?

That's when, once again, I decided to go with the (literal) flow. I didn't think of it as "Trying Softer" then, but that's what it was. That's what it always is when you don't fight against yourself.

Drawing strength from my pony experience, I consciously reconnected with my faith and turned this whole experience over to God. Even if my crying meant dying, I was OK. Whatever God had in store for me was what I would embrace.

The tears continued to flow all through the morning. I wondered how my tear ducts could hold so much water. Steady crying... steady crying... and constant soul-searching. I kept wondering where this might lead. On and off, I felt deep-seated fear.

Around 8:00, I grabbed my car keys and sneaked out of the house. I drove to a nearby lake, crying while driving. If only my eyes had possessed wiper blades! I pulled into a picnic area with a beautiful view of a calm lake. I shut off the motor, pulled the parking brake lever and merely sat.

By now I'd felt a rollercoaster ride of emotions. Many were painful. Thankfully, by around 10:00 a.m., I began to sense the subtle emergence of a deep-seated sense of strength. I couldn't tell where it came from, but it was there. At first, such a positive feeling was barely noticeable. It was obviously buried under a lot of stored-up pain. By this time, after about six hours of crying, my heart was doing a good job of offering reassurance. My mind, on the other hand, wasn't so confident.

By noon, I started to feel intermittent feelings of happiness. I was still crying, but I had an optimistic feeling. It was like knowing that behind the clouds, the sun is always shining. I even had a few brief flashes of joy.

I still didn't understand what the heck was happening, but whatever it was, I knew God was cracking my safe wide open. I knew he wanted me to find the treasure inside. And I was thankful. Even the notion that my crying episode was about a healing transformation caused my heart to swell with gratitude. Apparently, this whole experience was somehow a Gift from Spirit.

BUT THEN, just as I started to feel safe and blessed, I felt a horrible jab of fear and angst! I was shaken to the core!

The next thing I knew, whether it was a dream, delusion or vision, I don't know, but I could "see myself" standing in a dense forest! And directly in front of me, only a few yards away, was the entrance to a dreadfully scary-looking cave! In reality, of course, I was still in my car. But my consciousness had placed me in the woods, staring at this ominous cave. The cave was blocked by two huge and heavy boulders. I didn't know whether to be glad about that or fear the challenge I might have to face.

Everything in me hoped that the boulders were in place for my protection from some horrible creature. But *just then!!* Both rocks were moved off to the sides of the entrance! The big, gaping, dark cavern was wide open. There was nothing between me and whatever was in that cave! I felt immobilized. Actually terrified. Is this when I get eaten by some killer cave beast?

By this time, it was well past noon. I had been crying steadily for almost nine hours. Then I noticed that the safe (cave) door was wide open! Like it or not, ready for it or not, I was about to face whatever was lurking in this (my) inner sanctum.

Not to purposely hold you in suspense, (well maybe) but just to be totally honest about the circumstances and chain of events—at that very moment when something was about to emerge from the cave—I was transported back to a dream I'd had, some 40 years earlier. It happened when I was in my 20s. That dream is as follows:

It was a beautiful, sunny day. I had been happily working in the flowerbed outside of a little white-framed house. Not a care in the world. Without warning, something extremely dreadful and angry came charging around the corner of the house! It was set on killing me. I didn't know if it was a human, animal, alien or something else. But the feeling was evident. If it got me, I wouldn't exist anymore.

I dropped my garden tools and ran for my life. I ran toward the back of the house. I knew better than even to glance back. I didn't have to see it. It was enough for me to hear it, thunderously gaining ground. Whatever this thing was, it was faster than I. But that didn't mean I wasn't going to run until I could run no more. I wanted to live!

We raced around the house, probably 50 times. I was beyond exhausted. The situation was dire. I was depleted— out of energy, options, and even hope. Well... almost.

I decided (here we go again – to the ol' "Try Softer," surrender, move) to just turn around and face this monster head on! What the hell! What did I have to lose? If it was going to gobble me up, then that was just what would have to happen. At least I would go down fighting for all I was worth. I twirled around as fast as I could.

But here's the rub: so did the monster or demon, or whatever the creature was! The next thing I knew, I was running around the house in the other direction, with my attacker still viciously chomping at my heels. What had changed?

The "I" in my dream could forge no way to get this fearsome energy to not be after me. But even as I was preparing to face death, I couldn't bring myself to let go of hope. So, with angels carrying me, I kept going round and round the house.

On one pass of the front door, for what must have been the hundredth time, I glanced up toward the blue sky. Hanging from a large shade tree, I noticed a long, sturdy brown limb with green leaves on it. AH-HAA! I thought.

I willed my depleted body one last time around the house. Then when I was positioned directly under the big branch, with every ounce of strength remaining, I launched myself into the air and grabbed hold of the limb. Clinging to it for all I was worth, I pulled myself up, and into the safety of the lush branches of the big tree.

When I looked down, all I could see was the blur of some kind of evil thing running round and round the house, searching desperately for me. The thing was going so fast, I never did get a good look at it. Whatever it was, I knew it could not come up to my level to grab me. I knew I had, literally, risen above the problem. It all had been, albeit in nightmarish form, a profoundly healing dream-gift from me to myself. It was about the POWER OF TRANSCENDENCE.

In an instant, the old dream of tree-branch transcendence evaporated. I was relieved to see that I was still safe, just sitting in my car by the lake. But how safe? I was still having some kind of daydream experience or vision of a scary cave. And I was still weeping. How would I evade this cave monster? I could tell it was about to emerge! Oh My God! I thought. I can't run from this vision! I'm done for!

The next thing I knew, I felt the most loving feeling I ever remembered having. It was as though I was cradled in the heart of God. I suddenly understood that what had emerged from the cave was not any kind of dangerous animal. What was out of the cave, finally, was the sickest, most frightened part of me that I had kept locked inside, for who knows how long. The "monster" in the darkest part of my being was simply a belief. It was the false and debilitating, but somehow learned, belief that I was not lovable.

Insight flooded my being. I could see my own truth. And it was clear to me. What I had kept buried (locked in the bank vault of my soul) for so many years was the fear that I was not handsome enough, or adequate enough, or good enough, or man enough, or smart enough... to ever be loved by the woman of my dreams. That was the false belief that had blocked my spiritual alignment. But nine hours of tears and gentle "safe cracking" had cleared me out. I felt totally liberated! I felt free to be my authentic self. Judy's love had completely opened my heart.

I am lovable! I am lovable! I declared to myself. Whether I actually said it aloud, I don't know. What I did know was that FINALLY, my tears ceased.

Soon after my dramatic and self-imposed, (sponsored by my Higher Self, I mean) breakthrough, my wife and I agreed to divorce. It was as painful and difficult as any divorce, but a necessary growth event for both of us. Now that I was unblocked from myself, and more open than ever to allowing love to flow through me, I could no longer put myself or Rose through an unsatisfying relationship, one that was never going to go to the level of intimacy I needed. I was so sorry to have to leave but glad I was back on a healing path. More than glad. I felt deep gratitude to Judy for putting me in touch with my deepest self.

Though Judy had obviously been the catalyst for helping me find the strength to move on from an unhealthy relationship, I didn't leave Rose FOR her. As I said, Judy was already in a beautiful relationship with her true soulmate. And I knew he loved her with all his heart. He earned his living by tuning pianos. Music was in his soul... and his heart was as loving as Judy's. They made a perfect couple. I didn't want to, in any way, affect their relationship.

No. I left an unhealthy situation for my sake. It was a better relationship with myself that I was after and committed to attaining.

So there I was, in my late 60s, moving forward from a kind of "starting over" perspective. I committed to leaving it up to God to bring me my perfect partner. Whether that would ever happen wasn't as important to me as the knowledge that I had completely surrendered my life to God.

My stance, my way of being, my most authentic position in relationship to the Universe, now, and my personal commitment to myself, after my cathartic crying experience, was a simple one:

I promised God that henceforth, I was going to say YES to all things healthy and for my highest good, and NO to anything that would keep me from becoming my best version.

Thank God! (and Judy) that I was able to "Try Softer" enough to allow my most authentic self to emerge. Yes... I was born a dreamer and a horse lover. Yes... I was born to be a life coach and counselor. And yes... I was born to be an artist and an author. All of that I always found easy to accept. This time, it was the person underneath all of those roles, attributes and personality characteristics — the real me — that I finally, fully recognized and embraced.

There is no more real place for me to go to inside. The jig is up, the cat's outta the bag, and somewhere a fat lady was probably singing about it. The coast was clear. (Took a bunch of decades, but) FINALLY! I have met my true self.

Beyond that, I committed to honoring that essential part of my being, just the way God made me. I knew Judy was a true soulmate of mine. I knew she "saw" me and loved me for who I am. I felt my worth. And for the first time in many years, I felt worthy.

As Jonathan Lockwood teaches: "Great relationships begin with two people who are each self-confident and who come to each other with the openness to see and accept the other as a unique and wonderful person. If there is true love and an alignment of fundamental values, choose to join your life with your new partner and vow never to criticize their nature, the essence that makes them uniquely themselves."

Chapter 17

Better Safe than Sorry

"Trying Softer" means accepting that you are a precious child of God.

A Parable about Self-Worth

(Or maybe I should title it: Judy-the-Jeweler)

Once, a youth went to see a wise man, and said to him: "I have come seeking advice, for I am tormented by feelings of worthlessness and no longer wish to live. Everyone tells me that I am a failure and a fool. I beg you, Master, help me!"

The wise man glanced at the youth, and answered hurriedly, "Forgive me, but I am very busy right now and cannot help you. There is one urgent matter in particular which I need to attend to. But if you agree to help me, I will happily return the favor."

"Of course, Master!" muttered the youth, noting bitterly that yet again his concerns had been dismissed as unimportant.

"Good," said the wise man. He removed from his finger a small ring containing a beautiful gem.

"Take my horse and go to the market square. I urgently need to sell this ring to pay off a debt. Try to get a decent price for it, and do not settle for anything less than one gold coin. Go right now, and come back as quick as you can!"

The youth took the ring and galloped off. When he arrived at the market square, he showed it to the various traders, who at first examined it with close interest. But as soon as they heard that it would sell only in exchange for gold, they completely lost interest. Some of the traders laughed openly at the boy. Others simply turned away. Only one aged merchant was decent enough to explain to him that a gold coin was too high a price to pay for such a ring, and that he was more likely to be offered only copper or, at best, possibly silver.

When he heard these words, the youth became very upset, for he remembered the master's instruction not to accept anything less than gold. Having already gone through the whole market looking for a buyer, among hundreds of people, he saddled the horse and set off. Feeling thoroughly depressed by his failure, he returned to see the wise man.

"Master, I was unable to carry out your request. At best I would have been able to get a couple of silver coins, but you told me not to agree to anything less than gold! But the merchants told me that this ring isn't worth that much."

"That's a very important point, my boy," the wise man responded. "Before trying to sell a ring, it wouldn't be a bad idea to establish how valuable it really is. And who can do that better than a jeweler? Ride over to him and find out what his price is. Only don't sell it to him, regardless of what he offers you. Instead, come back to me straight away."

The young man once again leaped onto the horse and set off to the jeweler. The latter examined the ring through a magnifying glass for a long time and then weighed it on a set of tiny scales. Finally, he turned to the youth and said: "Tell your master that right now I can't give him more than 58 gold coins for it. But if he gives me some time, I will buy the ring for 70."

"Seventy gold coins!?" exclaimed the youth. He laughed, thanked the jeweler and rushed back at full speed to the wise man.

When the latter heard the story from the now animated youth, he told him: "Remember, my boy, that you are like this ring. Precious and unique! And only a real expert can appreciate your true value. So why are you wasting your time wandering through the market and heeding the opinion of any fool?"

To open yourself to life's natural riches, you need to first open yourself to how valuable you are. How perfect and priceless in the Universe in the eyes of God, Love, Life, and the Universe. You may not know this unless you are a doctor, but when all babies are born, they come out of their mother's womb with a sticker on the bottom of each foot. One says: "One of a kind, Made in Love" and the other says: "Priceless."

It's true! Yeah, honest, it's true! And peeling the stickers off doesn't change how forever precious, miraculous and invaluable each treasured human being is.

As you set out to delve into yourself, it may help to think of yourself as your own "safecracker." You won't need a stethoscope, black stocking mask or any disguise. Retrieving the parts of you locked away from the world is a matter of full disclosure. The only "crime" in picking the lock that keeps the REAL YOU encased and walled off within yourself would be not to release your authentic self into the world. In that case, you would rob everyone of the blessings of knowing the real you.

Whether you are a man or woman, old or young, rich or poor, to recover the greatest treasure on earth, which is "Your

Authentic Self" you must find a way into your own psyche. This means removing all things blocking your growth. Anything which makes you feel that you are unlovable is an obstruction to your happiness. Typical self-imposed barriers include fear, negative self-talk and self-image, and self-destructive behavior such as bad habits or addictions.

Unfortunately, feeling worthless and that you don't really matter is an all-too-common condition. Sometimes even the most (seemingly) happy-go-lucky people secretly suffer from such negative and depressive thoughts. The belief that you are not worthy of being happy is self-destructive in three major ways:

1) It sabotages your growth by keeping all things in your own best interest at arm's length.
2) It causes pain by blocking loving energy.
3) It makes you susceptible to various kinds of health problems.

The following exercise can help you gain a better sense of who you really are. Allow it to be a dance between you and your imagination. You are alone, not being judged or tested in any way. There is no right or wrong way to do, or even think about, this safe-cracking (soul-enhancing) exercise. Simply allow your mind to drift into gentle introspection. Allow the outer world to go on about its business without you. Be with yourself in silence. Just being silent is a healthy thing in itself.

Once you are relaxing comfortably in a private place where you can experience silence, allow your imagination to walk you through the following process gently:

1) First, recognize and honor your inborn desire to find and bring into the light of day, the "Treasure" (which is your Authentic Self) from its shadowy place of safekeeping. Most of what makes up the big, thick, impenetrable door of the "safe" you are trying to crack is fear. It's like one big, thick barrier of self-diminishing, negative-based beliefs, and fears. It's very effective at keeping joy from emerging into your life. Such a thick door, locked in place over many years, cannot be forced open. To uncover and meet your real self, force won't work. Instead, it will take the softer powers of will, confidence, intention, self-persuasion and self-direction and Love.

2) Turn the combination dial slowly and deliberately to hear the little tumblers lining up. Use both finesse and faith. For example, you might be gradually "turning the dial to the right" when suddenly you hear a voice inside say something like: "I guess I'm not all bad." Or "Maybe I actually am an OK person." Or "Perhaps I do have something to offer the world." Or "I guess it's possible that God loves me." These kinds of self-affirming thoughts and insights help you get closer to who you really are. Each time you hear that tumbler click because of a loving thought about yourself or others, you move closer to your ultimate goal of self-discovery. If you hear fear, doubt, hatred or any other kind of negativity arising within, then you need to gently "turn the numbers in the other direction" till they click again when they hit a positive realization.

3) Use more than good ears to hear your inner blocks being removed. You must listen with your heart if you expect to meet yourself again. Yes. You will need to align yourself with the energy of self-respect, self-appreciation, and ultimately self-love, even if you haven't felt any such positive energy throughout your entire life. It will help you to remind yourself, as you are trying to crack the safe, that the "you" inside is not the tiny, limited, powerless you that you have been conditioned to believe as the real you. No. The "you" inside the safe in the seat of your soul is miraculous, multi-dimensional, all loving, and all knowing. It is the God-essence of you. That is who we truly are when all earthly and egoistic dimensions are peeled away.

4) **Gently rotate the dial, listening for the little—sometimes loud, other times almost imperceptible—clicks telling you that you are gradually getting your ego-self and your own ideas about your personality out of the way.** You will easily be able to tell whether you are rotating the dial correctly. You can always tell by how you feel. If you feel a knot in your stomach while turning the dial, or anxiety about who you are, or fear that you might discover that you really are the unlovable person you always believed yourself to be, then you are not listening closely enough with your heart. Anytime you do not feel warm, comfortable or confident on this self-elected and directed journey to your highest self, it means your ego is distracting and blocking you. Fear and frustration, along with a convincing belief that you are not going to be able to succeed in getting more acquainted with yourself, are the ego's best weapons to keep you from finding "yourself." Use your heart, and its love light, to keep you on your path to a life worth living. The journey to everything good is a journey to your Heart.

5) **Be ready to cry.** Once you get that safe door open and catch even the first glimpse of yourself, the real you—so naturally and invincibly powerful in your vulnerability—tears of joy will come pouring out. These are cathartic and healing tears of the greatest happiness. There is no greater feeling than when you meet your truest, deepest, most authentic, highest self—your divine soul.

"Look at the birds of the air, that they do not sow, neither do they reap, nor gather into barns, and yet your heavenly Father feeds them. Are you not worth much more than they?" (Matthew 6:26)

Chapter 18

Find Quiet in Your Life

"Trying Softer" means diving deeply within.

Spritual teacher and master herbalist, Dr. Paul Haider has identified the following benefits of silence:

1. Silence helps you feel more like a human being, than a human doing.
2. Silence is good for the hormone-related systems in the body.
3. Silence boosts your immune system, making it easier for you to fight off dis-ease.
4. Silence contributes to your looking and feeling younger.
5. Too much noise can cause an increase in anxiety.
6. Your mind does more recharging when you are surrounded in silence than it does when you are sleeping.
7. Silence helps you calm yourself and feel more centered and balanced.

8. Silence boosts your brain chemistry, helping you feel happier and better able to focus.
9. Silence helps to reduce stress and lowers your adrenaline levels.
10. Silence can help reduce pain.

Relax into Patience

Once Buddha was walking from town to town with his followers. This was in the initial days. They happened to pass a lake, and Buddha told one of his disciples, "I am thirsty. Get me some water from that lake."

The disciple walked up to the lake and noticed that some people were washing clothes in the water. He also saw a bullock cart crossing through the lake. As a result, the water became very muddy, very turbid. The disciple returned to tell Buddha, "The water in there is very muddy. I don't think it is fit to drink."

After about half an hour, again Buddha asked the same disciple to go back to the lake and get him the water to drink. The disciple obediently went back to the lake. This time he found that the lake had absolutely clear water in it. The mud had settled, and the water above it looked fit to be drunk. He collected some water in a pot and brought it to Buddha.

Buddha looked at the water then looked up at the disciple and said, "See what you did to make the water clean. You let it be and the mud settled down on its own and you got clear water. Your mind is also like that. When it is disturbed, just let it be. Give it a little time. It will settle down on its own. You don't have to put in an effort to calm it down. It will happen effortlessly."

Buddha says having peace of mind is an effortless process. When there is peace inside you, that peace permeates to the outside. It spreads around you and into the environment.

Everyday Stress

Stress is part of life. In and of itself it is not a bad thing. As we go about our daily lives, we continuously experience both healthy and unhealthy forms of stress. Stress can come from the environment, our bodies and our thoughts. Positive stress is called "eustress." An example of positive stress is when we have a baby. Nothing could be more joyful, yet we instantly recognize our need to accept a lifelong increase in responsibility and a world of lifestyle changes. Good stress keeps us alert and involved in all of the important things in our life. Stress becomes negative when we are faced with continuous challenges without intermittent relief. When we get into "trying too hard" territory, and we become frustrated and overworked, tension builds to the point of causing problems.

Typical symptoms of too much negative stress include headaches, upset stomach, and elevated blood pressure. Chest pain and sleep disturbances are also common. Other stress-related symptoms may include heart problems, diabetes, skin conditions, arthritis, depression, and anxiety. Research indicates that the vast majority of all doctors' office visits (some studies say it rises as high as 90%) are for stress-related ailments and complaints. It's clear we all need to learn how to slow down, calm down, relax and "Try Softer." We all need to find some way, even for just a few minutes a day, to block out the crazy world and relax into our peaceful inner essence.

Any form of relaxation, if practiced regularly, can strengthen the immune system and produce a host of other health benefits for any of us, no matter what age, stage of life or circumstances we find ourselves in.

Have you noticed that when you mention the word "meditation" to some people, their eyes kind of glaze over? If you are not a regular meditator, yet really honest with yourself and highly tuned in to the subtleties of how you are feeling, it's likely that you will feel a slight increase in anxiety or defensiveness, just from entering this chapter. That's because meditation is one of your ego's least favorite words. If you really want to put someone on the defensive, say to them: "You should meditate."

Most of us understand and accept that meditation is a good and healthy thing to do. I've never heard of anyone complaining about being too relaxed, centered, happy and at peace. But because of so much ignorance about what it really is and so many claims as to how it has to be done, many people claim they either don't know how — can't control their thoughts — or they don't have time. No matter what the reason or excuse, not meditating is a great way to appease the ego. Appeasing the never-satisfied ego is not what "trying softer" is about.

"Trying softer" is about relaxing in every way — mentally, emotionally, physically and spiritually. Meditation is not only a wonderful way to unblock yourself and relax into alignment with your most authentic self, but it is the easiest way to do it. OK, the "easiest" way for some people. But if you want to, you can be one of those people. It's only a matter of choosing to meditate, in your own gentle way, on your own time schedule, and on your own terms. The notion that somehow meditation is some kind of mystical Eastern mind trip that you will not be able to control is bunk. There is nothing easier or more natural than meditation. You already do it all the time. Every time you find quiet in your life, you are meditating.

Therefore, I define meditation in its broadest sense. It simply means quieting your mind by focusing a little less on external stimuli. It doesn't mean blocking negative thoughts or even controlling anything about your thinking. In fact, being "lost in thought" can be a kind of meditation.

The beauty of meditation and the paradox of it is that it takes no effort. More than 20 years ago, I was trained in a specific technique called Transcendental Meditation. My teacher had worked with Deepak Chopra and had also taught Wayne Dyer the TM method. To this day, it is my preferred way to relax my mind. I tend to meditate several times each day, for short periods. I'm not rigid about it. Instead, I meditate whenever I want to slow myself down and get centered again. It is a wonderful tool, and it is truly effortless. The health benefits are numerous.

If you are sincerely interested in really slowing down your hectic lifestyle and reducing stress to the point where it stops managing you, I suggest you find a book or a teacher or investigate online the following kinds of proven methods of stress reduction:

Yoga: Ancient system of therapeutic postures for promoting mind/body/spirit integration.

Diaphragmatic Breathing: Easy method of learning how to allow each breath you take to reduce stress rather than contribute to it.

Guided Imagery: Uses visualization to achieve goals. May help with depression, high blood pressure, anxiety and pain management.

Self-Hypnosis: Teaches you how to self-induce a state of extreme relaxation in which you might experience a beneficial increase in susceptibility to suggestion, along with a heightened imagination.

Autogenic Training: A type of self-hypnosis that teaches you how to influence the regulation of bodily functions, such as heart rate, breathing, and blood pressure, that are normally regulated subconsciously.

Biofeedback: Enables you to monitor body functions, such as heart rate, brainwave state, skin temperature, and muscle tension, in real time, to see how effective your stress management is.

Progressive Muscle Relaxation: Involves alternating tensing and relaxing specific muscle groups, to change what can become an automatic kind of habitual cycle of stress-causing muscle tension in specific parts of your body.

Emotional Freedom Technique: Commonly referred to as "tapping." It is a form of acupressure involving stimulation with your fingertips at certain meridian points on your body.

Tai Chi: A popular Chinese martial art practiced for its defense training as well as its health benefits. It is a popular stress management system of slow and graceful body movements practiced in about 25 countries throughout the world.

Qi Gong: Like Tai Chi, combines slow, deliberate movements, meditation and breathing exercises to help with muscle tone, balance, circulation, and overall mind/body/spirit alignment.

Aromatherapy: A healing and relaxation technique incorporating the healing scents of essential oils.

Relaxing activities: Ordinary hobbies or creative outlets — such as woodworking or painting or even just listening to music — can help you maintain a more balanced and centered lifestyle. Fishing, hunting, running, biking, walking the dog — any kind of physical activity can be beneficial, including just playing outside and having fun.

Laughter: Truly can be the best medicine for improving your overall sense of well-being. It is nature's way of giving your internal organs a nice massage. Laughing with others is a beautiful experience of intimacy and commonality that promotes harmony and togetherness. It's hard to be angry, depressed or out of sorts while you have fun and laugh.

All of the above exercises and techniques for removing blocks and aligning yourself with your most authentic self involve mental relaxation. That's really all that meditation is. And the good news is you don't need to learn any specific way to meditate. Regardless of the many systems, methods, techniques, styles, and practices that have been developed, over thousands of years, how you meditate is entirely up to you. It can be fun to find your own, unique way. The bottom line is if it works for you it is "right."

If you choose to involve yourself in a regular system or practice of meditative healing exercises, that will be a powerfully healing action for you to do. I heartily recommend that you incorporate some kind of reflective practice into your everyday lifestyle. For myself, I can't imagine how I would have been able to lead such a fulfilling life if not for my daily practice with TM. But that was my choice. Think about what kind of choice makes the most sense for you, if you are interested in feeling better than you ever have before.

Burst of Love - Gift of Health

The following is an easy way to rejuvenate yourself whenever you want to. You don't need to invest a lot of time, find a special place, or wear any specific kind of clothing.

Nor or you required to bend your body into any particular postures. Of course, if you like, you can do any or all of those things. And to the extent you apply the techniques of any one of the popular stress-reducing techniques listed above, you are likely to receive increased health benefits. This is just a quick — still powerfully healing — (non)activity for those of us who are always on the go!

I suggest you read it over first to familiarize yourself with the three steps. Then, I trust, once you understand the sequence, you will be able to easily guide yourself through it.

Step 1) To begin, breathe normally, make yourself comfortable and close your eyes. You may sit or lie down in any position. Visualize a white light of spiritual energy surrounding and protecting you.

Relax and clear your mind. Allow all of your thoughts to be whatever and however they may be. There's no need to block them for this exercise, as they are a necessary part of the process.

Of course, if anything like mine, your thoughts will immediately go to amazingly creative and desperate lengths to gain your attention. Just accept that as perfectly normal and to be expected.

Whenever I think of freeing my thoughts to go wherever they want to, I imagine myself releasing a bunch of stall-bound, wild horses onto the freedom of an open range.

Step 2) Next, while your wild horses (thoughts) are galloping here, there and everywhere, relishing their freedom, picture yourself sitting on a soft bale of straw in the perfect barn.

Soon you are barely able to hear the distant horses. It is warm and cozy where you sit, perfectly private and safe. There's even a golden ray of sunlight caressing the edge of your straw seat.

The only thought that even halfway grabs your attention now is the surprising realization that you can't recall the last time you felt so comfortable.

Take three long and slow, deep and deliberate, breaths. Then relax back into normal breathing. As your heart fills with reverence, gently repeat the following words to yourself over and over again.

Say them continuously and consciously, in whatever rhythm feels the most natural to you. Feel the eternal beauty and profound truth of all that you are reminding yourself of.

Repeat this sacred phrase as often as you like:

I am the peace of God.... I am the peace of God.... I am the peace of God...

Step 3) Continue communing with your true nature for as long as you like. Trust your intuition on timing. Twenty minutes of this kind of meditation is probably optimal, but even if you do it for only one minute, you will give yourself a priceless gift. When you are ready, slowly open your eyes. Very gently and gradually allow yourself to come back to a normal waking state. Don't rush to stand up.

Lovingly allow your "horses" to return to any corral you might want them in, taking care to always keep them healthy and in good spirits.

The moment you see yourself opening the gate to set your thunderous herd of wild thoughts free, a Burst of Love is released.

The moment you even consider the truth that your essence is the Peace of God, your being lights up with increased inner peace and harmony.

This kind of inward focus is, in and of itself, a profound expression of self-respect. Whether you call it meditation, relaxing, taking a break or time out, or just claiming some "me time," the healing effects of honoring yourself in stillness are many and great.

"*Sometimes, simply by sitting, the soul collects wisdom.*"
— Zen Proverb

It's an indescribably wonderful feeling to find yourself floating in the kind of divine inner space that getting in touch with the essence of your soul provides. One might ask then: But what is the best, most personally healing, way for us to conduct the rest of our lives, during the vast majority of moments when we are not meditating?

To answer, I would remind and assure you that because you are a spiritual being having a human experience, and not the other way around, you are never away from your inner house of worship. You can't leave your heart. You can block it, deny it, pretend it is of no importance, but just as blood always courses through your veins, your heart's truth and guidance always flow through your being. Just like you get physically stronger by exercising your muscles, when you meditate you become more integrated, compassionate, healthy and content by allowing your heart to "pump you up."

To the extent you can let go of fear and embrace your true self, your realness and your vulnerability, your spirituality and soulful vitality will become stronger. Stronger in easy blossoming and exuding love—hence, more powerful.

Mind/Body/Spirit Benefits of "Trying Softer"

1) Improving relationships: The first relationship you will improve by slowing down and allowing time for self-reflection is the relationship with yourself. Taking time to balance yourself with a couple of slow, deep breaths and relaxing into a feeling of centeredness also helps to improve your relationships with others. When you are better able to manage your emotions, you are less likely to say something that you may regret later, and you can present yourself with more authenticity and genuine presence.

2) Gaining a better perspective: Allowing plenty of time to gather your thoughts rather than instantly jumping to conclusions helps you see the big picture. Such an unhurried pace enables you to do more musing and pondering. In the long run, spending time to fully appreciate your circumstances and options helps you avoid mistakes and saves time that might otherwise be wasted by acting too hastily.

3) Slowing down self-chatter: Quieting your mind—whether it be through some form of structured meditation or simply just relaxing with yourself, eyes closed and thinking about nothing—does wonders for your busy brain. Mental relaxation can be even more rejuvenating than physical rest. Begin to do less wrestling with your internal self. When you start to feel anxious, allow your thoughts to come and go, just to flow through you.

4) Smelling the roses: When you relax into the present moment, your senses become more alive. When you eat, you can taste your food more. When you look around, you can appreciate the colors in your environment. When your stress level is reduced, you are better able to enjoy all of the sights, sounds, scents, and textures of nature.

5) Making fewer mistakes: By not hurrying too much through your day, all tensed up and stressed, you will be less likely to make poor judgments and regrettable mistakes. Being relaxed mentally helps you remember to do wiser and more prudent things, such as "measure twice, cut once."

6) Being a better friend/partner/spouse: To the extent you can slow down and center yourself, you will be better able to think before you speak and consciously remember to listen respectfully to your loving partner. Given that you can share only that which you have, if all you have is anxiety, stress, fear, and tension, then that's all you can share with your loved ones. If you have contentment and a healthy, relaxed attitude, then you will be able to share that kind of love.

7) Making better decisions: Sometimes when we make short-sighted decisions, or what turn out to be wrong decisions, it is because we are too stressed to think straight. Anxiety is like a fog that blurs our judgment. By relaxing, going a little easier on ourselves, we can get a clearer sense of what we want to do in every situation. Also, being mentally relaxed enables us to consider all of the options, and avenues of choice, before making critical decisions.

8) Becoming a better communicator: Many, if not most, of the world's problems are caused by miscommunication. Life gets a lot easier when we are able to express ourselves with clarity. When you are relaxed and focused, and not putting pressure on yourself, you can become more accurately aware of what you want to express to someone in any situation. Your communication becomes more natural and authentic. That's when lots of potential misunderstandings and conflicts can be headed off.

9) Enjoy everything more: Babies naturally live in the present moment. When they are eating, that's all they are doing. When they cry or play, then that is what they are doing, and what all of their senses and focus attend to. The challenge for us oldsters is to relax enough to enjoy every activity, no matter how mundane. The more stressed out you are, the less likely that becomes possible.

10) Get off the merry-go-round: Some call it "the rat race." Others talk about the "dog-eat-dog" world. For many of us, it does seem that we are victimized by such a fast-paced world, that we have no control over how we spend our time. Many of us feel overworked and overwhelmed much of the time. Next thing we know, our short life is coming to an end and all we did was race from one thing to the next. The antidote is to find a way of taking care of yourself first. I'm not talking about being selfish. I just mean that you might have to say "no" a little more often. Merry-go-rounds are supposed to be fun. Allow yourself to enjoy the ride by learning how to relax into your natural self by practicing a little self-nurturing.

11) Not just developing, but actually appreciating patience: How often have you heard someone say: "Boy do I love being patient." I know the answer to that. Never! We all know how hard it is to delay gratification. The key to learning, at least how to be somewhat more patient, is to realize that nothing happens before its time. No matter how eager you are to see the colored petals, the flowers you plant in the spring can't blossom any faster than they do. By slowing down your lifestyle, reducing anxiety, and smelling the roses, you learn that the time you spend waiting for something to happen doesn't have to be wasted. You will feel freer to joyfully fill those precious moments with anything you can think of for your highest good.

12) Allowing others to help you: It's a cool thing to be a do-it-yourselfer. And it is very rewarding. That is the way most hobbyists, craftsmen, and artists need to function. Many activities require solo energy. That can be private time, and alone time, wonderfully spent. But some of us take that "I can do it myself" attitude to extremes. We isolate ourselves, run into problems and then feel too proud to ask for help. We forget that it's never a sign of weakness to ask for assistance.

In fact, the strongest words anyone can say are "Please help me." Put yourself in the shoes of the one being asked to help another. Don't you instantly respect that person? And doesn't it feel great to oblige? Don't miss out on sharing (anything and everything) when you have a chance.

13) Becoming better at sports: If you like to participate in a sports activity, you will probably get more out of it (meaning have more fun) if you put less ego and extra exertion into it. In other words, trying too hard to kick, hit or catch the ball, or whack it with a paddle without keeping yourself centered and your mind focused and relaxed will most likely impede your success. You golfers know exactly what I am talking about.

14 Becoming a better musician: One of the most common directives music students hear from their teachers is "Let's try that again. Take it a little slower this time." Especially when learning something new, like a language or a musical instrument, it helps to take baby steps at first. In music, such things as intonation, stamina, accuracy, and mindfulness are better learned by "trying softer" at times.

15) Becoming a better pet owner, not to mention parent: Here again, patience is key. We all learn at one point or another, and usually the hard way, that coercing a child or a pet, or any other living thing, to do what we want them to by use of fear or force tends to backfire ultimately. A relaxed, kind, focused and persistent approach always works better. When you approach others with high anxiety, they automatically become defensive. Conversely, when you are more centered and serene yourself, you will inspire connection and cooperation.

16) Getting a better handle on bad habits and addictions: Habits, good or bad, are matters of choice. Theoretically at least, a person can choose to quit a habit. But addiction, by definition, has a psychological/physical component that makes it very difficult, if not impossible, for a person to control without help. In both cases, and all other forms of self-defeating or self-harming behavior, it is generally helpful for individuals to slow down their impulses and behavior to a point where they may become more conscious of their "chosen" actions. This can be achieved through relaxation techniques such as biofeedback and meditation. Once people gain more self-control and function with less anxiety and stress, they are better able to learn how to help rather than hurt themselves by their actions.

17) Enjoying better health: Most health experts agree that a strong connection exists between our mental and psychological state and our physical health. When we feel depressed, stressed or emotionally worried or drained, we become more likely candidates for dis-ease. Typical symptoms include tension, pain in shoulders and back, fatigue, heart palpitations, raised blood pressure, poor sleeping patterns and even a suppressed immune symptom.

18) Greater peace of mind: "Trying softer" means taking time out to relax mentally as well as physically. As mentioned, you don't have to do any kind of formalized meditation. Instead, just sit quietly with yourself for 15 to 20 minutes, twice a day. It will help to make sure you have privacy, sit or lie down comfortably, close your eyes and think only of your breathing, while all other thoughts float in and out of your mind. Just a little self-care, a couple times a day, can make a world of difference in your daily mood, confidence level, and greater sense of self-worth.

19) Becoming more compassionate and contributory: When you take good care of yourself by managing your pace and stress levels you feel better about yourself. As your levels of self-respect and positive regard go up, so will your empathy and compassion toward others. When we like who we are, we tend to want to help others feel better about themselves. That often leads to such beautiful things as random acts of kindness.

Chapter 19

The Spirit of the Horse

"Trying Softer" means opening the doorway to your inner world.

When I was ten, a pony named Lucky validated my faith. Because I'd always felt she had been calling to me in the spiritual realm, I knew that finding her would not be a matter of luck. Rather, even as a child, I understood in my soul that to bring her to me, I needed to completely honor my heart's desire, longing and knowing. My methodology wasn't magical or mystical. It was simply to "Try Softly" enough not to block that which was mostly good for me. I always acted "as if" my pony was coming to me. What nobody around me seemed to understand was that I wasn't acting.

When you "Try Softer," you open the doorway to your inner world. This is the land of intuition, emotion, sensory information, heart wisdom, and your soul's voice. Horses live in this territory of openness. They are always conscious—not only about what's going on with each member of the herd, but also with humans.

When you stand near horses, they instantly read you, like a member of the herd. They can tell whether you are in spiritual alignment. If you are cocky, they know it… if you are afraid, they feel it… if you are angry, they sense it immediately. If you are kind and mean them no harm, they will understand that. Though they may appear to be big, muscle-bound brutes (although if you look in their eyes, you can't miss their sublime spirituality), they are actually more sensitive than most humans can fathom.

Horses need to be fully conscious and aware because their well-being depends on knowing the emotional state of every member of their herd. They don't judge any emotion to be better or worse than any other. Instead, they accept the authenticity of every feeling any one of them has in any given moment.

They read humans in the same way. Unlike many of us, they don't stuff emotions or hide their feelings. If they have emotional baggage, say from past abuse, they reveal it in unedited ways. The thoughts and feelings of a horse are clean, clear, real, honest and always in the present moment. Concerning their uncomplicated realness and total involvement with life in every present moment, they actually practice their version of the three principles of Loving allowance… Increased communication… and Self-responsibility better than most humans. Regarding simply being their authentic self, like most animals, they are always in a natural "Try Softer" mode. They know what it feels like to be emotionally free. These qualities, and so many more, are why horses are so good for humans.

I didn't grow up analyzing horses or spending a lot of time wondering why they were good for me; I grew up just loving them. They are in my blood. Spiritually, I can't separate myself from them. Yet because my life was so consumed with painting, counseling, working around the house and doing normal family things, I hadn't been around horses for half a century. In fact, as you will soon read, when they finally came back into my life, I was intimidated by their imposing size and power.

Hitting the trail on my own

After my divorce, I moved into a suitable apartment near my friend Bonnie. It was a nice country apartment in a remodeled barn. It was a one-bedroom, three-floor condo that featured a brick floor with a fireplace on the lower level. There were wooden beams across the ceiling, plenty of windows, and new carpet on the steps and in the bedroom. It was perfect for my taste and needs. I set up housekeeping on my own. I designated the bottom floor as a combination kitchen and studio.

Though the divorce and subsequent move were painful and difficult, I managed to adjust fairly well. While most of my contemporaries were in winding-down mode and planning their next golf outing, I was starting over. Because of my self-employed status, I had saved only a minimal amount of retirement money. The challenge was going to be not to use it. Instead, I needed to try and get by on my social security income, plus whatever painting sales I could bring in. Whatever might be in store for me, I was ready to accept. Having opened myself up to the real me, I felt strong in faith, soul-inspired and motivated. I was ready for my next "pony."

Though I couldn't imagine how it would happen, my heart was finally open to finding the woman of my dreams to share my life. It occurred to me that somehow, someday, Judy might be that person. But I also knew better than to change my life "for her." I knew I had to make this transition for myself. Most importantly, I completely respected the fact that she was already in a fulfilling relationship, and I didn't want to interfere in that beautiful union. By this time along my life's journey, I had learned enough about relationships to know that the only person I needed to work on, ever, was myself. I also knew that happiness comes from within, not from another person.

Thankfully, I had lots of friends, and a totally supportive family to help me adapt to my new way of living. Of course, my two children, Ben and Amanda, were completely loving and supportive. They helped me, almost in a role-reversal kind of way. One example of what I mean is that instead of me helping them to set up their college dorms, they helped their senior citizen old man set up housekeeping. Both of my brothers and their spouses were equally supportive. Larry and Joy always knew what to say to lift my spirits. And Randy and his wife Lorraine went way beyond the call of duty to help me get settled on my new path.

I am so blessed to have such a wonderful family!

I had committed to living the way of the horse. That's the "Try Softer" way of always being honest with myself, and everyone else, about who I am and how I'm feeling.

Before I left Rose, I had pledged to God that henceforth, I would always say "YES" to those things (relationships, circumstances, opportunities, dreams, etc.) that are clearly for my highest good. Conversely, I would never again hide or diminish myself in any relationship. Nor would I settle for a partner who did not fully appreciate and love me for who I am. The nine-hour crying episode had unblocked me to the point where I had become my most authentic self, and that's whom I was going to honor.

The Beat of the Drum

As I was getting set up to live on my own, Judy continued enjoying her life with Chris. They shared a beautiful stone farmhouse in the country. As I already mentioned, they were the gentlest of spirits dedicated to helping others become better versions of themselves. And one of their favorite, most rewarding, shared activities was conducting drum circles.

Drumming is an ancient musical tradition that many cultures around the world use to energize and build self-confidence. They are organized events where people sit in a circle with "djembe" drums in front of them. Drum circles are wonderfully therapeutic, rhythmic exercises giving a gathering of individuals the experience of being a part of a group.

A djembe (or jembe) is a skin-covered, goblet-shaped drum played with the bare hands. These instruments originated in West Africa.

Judy and Chris had been conducting drum circles for many years. In fact, they had become fairly well-known throughout a four-state area for bringing therapeutic drumming into nursing homes, schools and also in city squares during special events for the public. Their favorite venue was working with special-needs children.

Whenever and wherever Judy and Chris set up their circle of drums, everybody was welcomed to try their hand (literally) at playing a djembe. They always created a relaxed and safe environment in which even someone new at drumming felt comfortable. You didn't need to be a musician, or even have any sense of rhythm, to join in. Additionally, they always had other percussion instruments available for participants. These included instruments such as maracas, tambourines, hand drums, and gourds. Because both Chris and Judy were non-judgmental, kind and inviting, as well as talented, there was never an empty seat behind any of their drums. They just wanted to spread joy.

One day, after I'd been on my own for several months, I received a concerning call from Judy. "I think Chris has something going on. I'm not sure, but I feel it is some kind of serious health problem." She went on to say that the only basis she had for feeling as she did was her intuition. But I knew how in tune she always was with everybody and everything. That's just who she was.

Judy (known as "Jute" when she was drumming) was very beautiful. Her divine femininity, her physical beauty, the kindness of her heart and her sweet personality added up to the total gift you received when in her presence. When she and Chris did their drumming, she always wore the most creative, handmade, beautifully colored dresses and jewelry you can imagine. She was a celebration of all that is beautiful and spiritual.

Chris and Judy were in their late 50s by this time. They were admired by everyone. I always thought their combined mission of bringing people together by primal, rhythmic drumming was both compelling and therapeutic.

In my new life, Judy and I continued our special friendship and studying the *Gene Keys* together. As I'm sure you can understand, I always looked forward to her visits. They weren't every week, but fairly often. One day when Judy stopped by, I could tell she was bothered by something major. I knew it had nothing to do with me, or with Chris being jealous of me. I was his friend too. He understood and supported that Judy and I were connected spiritually, but not in any romantic way. Within seconds, she began crying. "Chris was diagnosed with fourth-stage colon cancer."

I can't remember how many months went by before Chris passed, but I think it was less than six. He had chosen not to get treatment. Judy remained by his side, nursing him sweetly, from the moment he was diagnosed until he took his last breath. Thankfully, her boss at her job at a local fitness center was kind enough to allow Judy to be with Chris as much as she needed to, without fear of losing her employment.

From the beginning of Chris's decline, Judy would call me regularly for support. I did what I could to help both of them. That meant little more than listening with an open and understanding heart.

At one point, before he passed, Chris and Judy had been scheduled to conduct a drum circle at a community theater for a large group of children. Because Chris wasn't feeling up to it at the time, they asked me if I would take his place.

I humbly agreed. With Judy's guidance and help from her sister, the drumming session worked out well.

After Chris died, Judy found herself needing a new place to live. (Non)coincidently there was a single-unit vacancy in the carriage house next to my apartment. One thing led to another, and we became neighbors.

Living within 50 feet of each other was a great comfort to both of us. I was trying to establish a healthy life as a soulfully-healed man, accepting whatever God had in store for me. She was trying to move forward while grieving the devastating loss of the love of her life.

We did a beautiful job, I must say, of gently supporting each other by sharing many cups of tea, lots of good meals, long walks, and hours of healing conversations. We used both the *Gene Keys* book and "Heart IQ" wisdom in every therapeutic way we could find. We were two spiritual seekers, each a tad lost, and each caring for the other. We were there for each other, yet respectful enough to give the other space and privacy.

Judy decided she wanted to keep up the drum circle tradition in honor of Chris. She invited me to help her with several prescheduled drum-circle commitments. I was happy and honored to join her in that wonderfully therapeutic process. I grew to love drumming too.

I never even thought of it as taking Chris's place. That would have been impossible because he was an exceptional person. Besides, Judy and I both knew he was still drumming with us in spirit. Instead, we developed our own style, which, of course, was always as therapeutic for us as it was for our participants.

Respecting Judy's need to grieve and heal, I was always careful not to push our relationship in a particular direction. She appreciated that and felt the same way about not steering us in any direction. We had a wonderfully balanced relationship—full of potential—and had no intention of messing it up. My heart always sang in her presence. It was great to have her living next door. I remember lots of pleasant evenings walking by her apartment and hearing her playing and singing for herself on Chris's piano.

On the other side of my apartment, I also had my wonderful friend Bonnie (Yes, the same Bonnie who had introduced me to Judy). Clearly, divine orchestration was happening all over the place!

I felt so happy in my relationship with Judy that one evening after we got back from an Italian restaurant, I gave her the little heart I'd found in the field. She cried. She happily accepted my gift as a symbol, not only of our soul connection, but also in recognition of how God had brought us together.

Judy

One day, another friend of mine, Kay, called me. She knew I was living alone and still recovering from my divorce. She was concerned about how I was doing. "You know I read your book, Tom," she said. "And like you, I love horses too. Guess what! I have one now!"

Kay went on to explain that she had adopted a rescued horse that had been injured while pulling an Amish buggy. The horse, Autumn Joy, wasn't physically injured but suffered major psychological trauma. The Amish owner had decided to get rid of her. Even though Kay was not an experienced horse person, she stepped in to rescue the chestnut Standardbred. Kay then asked: "Would you like to meet AJ?" She said she was boarding her new horse at a nearby farm.

The invitation landed right in my heart. Except on a couple of occasions, I hadn't been around horses for decades. But I'd always continued to read horse stories and magazines as well as watch every movie ever made about horses. Over the years, I had even painted several images of horses. A couple of those paintings were commissioned portraits. "Yes," I replied. "Thank you, Kay. I'd love to meet AJ."

Kay picked me up an hour later, and we drove to the barn where she boarded her horse.

We arrived at the picturesque farm nestled on 30 acres of rolling hills in Southeast Pennsylvania. The 19th-century farmhouse was charming. It wasn't a big house, but it was built with caring and creative craftsmanship. It was a light yellow frame house with a stone foundation. It featured a reddish colored roof. The country residence also had lots of windows and a porch off both the front and back. The rooms on the first floor featured really cool, wide windowsills. The house was beautifully landscaped, tastefully surrounded by various kinds of flowers, bushes and shade trees.

There were three barns on the property: one mid-sized bank barn, one big arena barn, and one small, five-stall middle barn that also featured a workshop and tractor shed. There were wood-fenced paddocks everywhere, purposely laid out so that every horse had access to freshly flowing drinking water from the property's natural streams. The whole scene — with the rustic, gray barn siding and red tin roofs — was idyllic, especially with the addition of over 20 multi-colored horses grazing throughout the property.

The co-owner (along with her husband) of the farm met us at the main gate. Jane was an energetic, pretty and petite horsewoman with wild, curly hair. She welcomed us warmly. She immediately offered me a tour of the property.

I got to meet AJ, as well as several other rescued horses. Equally wondrous, I got to pet goats, donkeys, a llama, and an alpaca. Well… not the alpaca. "Higgy" was a little too skittish for me to approach.

The atmosphere of the farm felt healing to me. Honestly, I felt as though I was "home." I can't explain it any more accurately. I felt completely welcomed.

Kay and I stayed for about two hours. Just as we were about to leave, Jane turned to me. "Kay said that you are an artist, right?"

I replied that I was. I told Jane that I'd been thinking about painting a farm animal with a Santa's hat for an upcoming Christmas exhibit.

"I have exactly what you need!" Jane said excitedly. Then she turned and ran toward the farmhouse. "Don't go yet. I'll be right back!"

When she came out of the house, she handed me a photo she had taken the previous Christmas. It was an image of one of her goats wearing a Santa hat!

"Wow! That's perfect!" I exclaimed. "May I borrow it to use as a reference? I'll bring it back in a couple of days."

"Sure. Keep it as long as you want. Feel free to come back to the farm any time. You can hang out with all of the animals and take as many pictures as you like."

Upon hearing such a beautiful invitation, my eyes welled with tears. Jane's kind words were healing to my heart. To my soul, they felt like an invitation for the ultimate horse lover to come home to his horses. I left the farm feeling great joy. I thanked Kay for connecting me with a place that, I somehow knew, was going to reconnect me with myself.

*Photo of my Christmas
miniature goat painting*

Life at the Horse Farm

I started going to the barn every day. Since I was retired, I had the time. It really felt good to help Jane with the farm work. Fortunately, I was still in good enough shape to do it. It was obvious that she needed and fully appreciated help with the chores.

Jane did a great job of running the farm. She rescued, cared for and trained horses, taught riding lessons (including to special-needs kids) and ran a successful horse-boarding business. At the time of my first visit, the farm had 25 horses. Jane was amazingly creative in her own right. She was like a female MacGyver, always figuring out how to make things work. One minute she would be cleaning stalls, the next minute she might be up in a loft throwing down hay.

The next thing you know, you'd find her grooming a horse, washing one or working one in the round pen. It wouldn't be unusual for her to do all of that, and a bunch of other chores, before clipping a goat's hoof, fixing a downed fence board, and driving off — a horse trailer in tow — to win another riding competition at a local horseshow. While Jane's thing was horses, her husband worked in, loved, and taught all areas involving media production. He was a highly regarded and successful expert in all areas of radio and TV broadcasting.

Going to the farm every day and helping Jane became my fulltime (voluntary) job. She was always patient with me — treated me as a new farm hand. She could tell that as much as I loved horses, I was unsure of myself around them. She said that I would overcome that fear just by being around them every day. I could see right away that I was going to learn everything I needed to know by watching how she behaved with them. Jane was a natural-born horse whisperer.

One of her favorite horses at the time was a Paso Fino named Cisco. The following story, about Cisco's journey, helped me better understand how we always need to "Try Softer" around these sensitive animals. Here's the heart-warming tale of how she trained Cisco.

Cisco

The Paso Fino is a naturally-gaited, light horse breed originally imported from Spain. They are prized for their smooth gait. They are used in many disciplines but are especially popular for trail riding. Jane had always wanted a Paso.

It all started when a lady from Maryland had several horses she could no longer take care of. The herd included stallions, mares, and foals of various breeds, including a few Paso Finos. She had been going from farm to farm looking for people to take some of her horses. When one of Jane's friends heard about the Maryland woman's quest, she called Jane to see if she might want to take a Paso.

At the time, Jane thought a Paso might be an ideal horse for her father. She had been on the lookout for a couple of years for such a gentle horse for him. Because her father was approaching 90, all that mattered was its gentleness.

One day Jane drove to Maryland to visit the lady's farm. After greetings, she and the owner walked into a beautiful pasture filled with horses. Of all the horses there, Cisco was the only one to come near Jane. He walked right up to her on his own accord. He was naturally drawn to her. But he wouldn't let her touch him. The lady shared that Cisco was 10 and had just been gelded. She added that he had been a stud, never ridden and not even halter broken. In other words, he was a completely wild horse. That was all Jane needed to hear. She could never pass up a challenge to work with a difficult horse, especially one she felt so instantly connected to.

Using her horse-whispering ways, Jane loaded Cisco into the trailer. She brought him home and put him in a safe stall. From that point on, Jane was careful about how she handled this wild horse. She advised everyone to steer clear of Cisco until she could help him adjust.

At first, each time Jane entered his stall, Cisco would instantly turn his rear toward her. Then he would jam his head into the corner and freeze with fear. Apparently, this was not going to be a good horse for her aging father. No. This was a horse that, unless somebody could train him with a "Try Softer" approach, was likely to end up hurting himself or someone else. That could result in the necessity to put this beautiful animal down.

But Jane trusted the deep connection she felt to her new Paso. She sensed that with enough love and patience, she could eventually work with Cisco. He seemed like a special animal.

Jane's initial strategy was to go into Cisco's stall and just sit there. She did that, and nothing else, for a couple of weeks.

Gradually, she was able to touch the horse gently with a brush. Not long after that, she was able to get a halter on him. Jane remained cautious about each move she made. If she raised her hand, even slightly, to touch him or to put a halter on him, Cisco would spin around, put his rear end toward her and jam his head back into a corner of the stall. Fortunately, he wasn't a kicker.

It took months of patience, bonding, trust-building, and round-penning before she attempted to get on Cisco. But, eventually, using natural horsemanship techniques, Jane was gradually able to slide herself onto Cisco's bare back. The first time she got on him, Cisco took a few steps and then suddenly reared straight up. Jane instinctively grabbed hold of his mane to keep herself from sliding off. She dismounted as soon as he came down and settled a bit. For several months, this was the pattern every time she mounted her spirited, obviously traumatized Paso.

Jane eventually got Cisco to the point where she was able to ride him, even with a saddle. He rarely bucked, the way you would picture a wild bronco jumping. But every so often, Cisco would resort to that dangerous (for both horse and rider) habit of suddenly rearing up. And each time he did, he would stretch straight up, like a Hollywood stunt horse.

Over time, Jane realized that whenever Cisco reared up, he acted as if there was an invisible wall in front of him. It was like a wall of fear, somehow, that he would not move through. No matter what she tried—whether different saddles, different riding environments, or even bringing in a horse chiropractor—Cisco just kept hitting his invisible wall. Recognizing that her horse was blocked by fear, perhaps from some past trauma, Jane decided to call in our amazing animal acupuncturist friend, Patti.

When Patti initially met Cisco, her first comment was, "His eyes are veiled. They have a kind of film over them." Jane acknowledged she'd noticed the dullness too. "Let's see if we can remove the blocks that are keeping him in such fear," the acupuncturist said.

Jane stood quietly beside her beloved Paso, as Patti inserted the needles in all the right spots on the horse's body. Soon Cisco lowered his head and began licking motions with his tongue. "That means it's working!" Patti assured Jane.

Jane smiled and gently put her hand on Cisco's neck. "Good boy."

Instantly, Jane's whole body felt as if she was receiving an electrical shock!

If you've ever seen the movie *The Green Mile* you will easily be able to picture what happened next.

Cisco, somehow telepathically, transferred all of his thoughts and emotions to Jane. However that happened, it happened. And Jane started to weep. Then weeping became sobbing. With her hand still on Cisco's neck, she could see (feel, know and understand) the painful history of the abused horse's earlier life. It was made clear to Jane's conscious awareness that this beautiful Paso had been searching for her for years. He "told" her that he had suffered a very painful past. That he'd been starved and forced to compete for food with 36 horses on just seven acres. That he was used for breeding only and was frequently beaten with a cane by the cruel man who owned him. All of that information was psychically transferred from Cisco's spirit to Jane's heart.

Overwhelmed with empathy, she cried for several minutes over her new horse's deep pain.

The acupuncture treatment had certainly worked to unblock this great horse. Within minutes, his eyes were bright and shiny. From that day forward, Cisco gradually became more and more cooperative and dependable. It still took a few more years to get Cisco to the point where he was reliably trained, to the point of not rearing.

Eventually, the love and trust between horse and rider were so solid that Jane went on to show her beloved Paso, and win ribbons in various kinds of horse competitions. He was her horse, for sure.

After hearing that part of Cisco's story, and witnessing firsthand the magic of how the two of them related to each other, in time, I too formed a bond with this noble animal.

I had grown up knowing that horses are highly spiritual creatures; that's how I always connected with them as well. My pony story is all about that. But seeing how it works between a horse and its loving owner in everyday life, at this amazing level, was both enlightening and healing to me.

Photo of Jane riding Cisco

Annabelle

One day Kay called Jane to tell her about another pony that needed to be rescued. Kay had learned of a family that had a

Bashkir Curly pony that they couldn't handle. They said they were about ready to put the pony down. The owners said that the pony was so dangerous they were even afraid to enter her stall. Kay assured Jane that she wasn't trying to get her to take a dangerous horse. Rather, she felt that this pony was misunderstood and mislabeled.

Jane and I scheduled an appointment with the owners. Then we drove to their farm. Upon arrival, we went straight to the stall to see the white pony. Curly ponies are very distinct in their appearance. Her hair was like a poodle's. This pretty pony had blue eyes and was curly all over.

In our presence, the owner couldn't wait to prattle down her list of all the things bad or wrong about this bad pony, including:

*She is unpredictable and dangerous...
*She doesn't like men...
*If you get in the stall she will push you and pin you...
*She can't be ridden...
*You can't trim her feet...
*You can't lunge her...
*She bites and kicks...
*And you'll never be able to get her on a horse trailer.

After hearing so many indictments, Jane and I both thought that maybe this pony was too much for us to handle. But we hated even the possibility that she would be killed rather than cared for. She wasn't even that old. We also agreed that she just didn't look, or act, like the wild beast we were being told she was.

But, we wondered, why would the owner lie about such a thing? Reluctantly concluding that she should err on the side of safety, Jane decided that Annabelle would be too much of a disruptive force on the farm. It was a painful decision for her to reach. I could tell she was torn in her heart about what to do. I didn't have any strong sense either way, other than I kept feeling that the woman wasn't describing the true nature of this little white pony. Then again, it wasn't my place to even suggest to Jane what horses to bring or not bring to her farm. We thanked the people and said we were sorry but would have to pass on taking their pony.

The next morning when I came to the farm, Jane was waiting at the gate. "I hardly slept at all last night." Her eyes began to fill with tears. "Annabelle came to me in a dream. She told me she has been waiting for me to save her from this family who couldn't understand her at all. I woke up literally sobbing. I had the most powerful longing to bring her here. My husband asked me what was wrong. When I explained everything, he said if I wanted her that badly, I should go get her. So wanna take a ride?"

"I'm ready!" I replied.

"Good. I'll call ahead and let them know we're coming. You mind throwing down some hay till we're ready to go?"

I must admit I was a little surprised by her change of mind. But I had already learned that when it came to reading horses, nobody was more in touch with the mysterious equine Spirit than Jane.

We hitched up the trailer and headed to the wild white pony's farm. Upon arrival, the owner took us directly to Annabelle's stall. You could tell she was happy that we were taking her pony. And I'm sure she was relieved not to have to put "Curly" down.

With no hesitation, Jane calmly entered the beast's stall. Annabelle showed no signs of even being anxious. She stood quietly as my horse-whisperer friend put a lead rope on her. Then Jane calmly led the bad-girl pony out of the stall and straight onto the trailer. No problem.

Once back at the farm, Annabelle backed easily out of the trailer. We put her in a centrally located holding paddock. There she could meet other horses over the fence and yet still be isolated a bit until she got accustomed to her new home.

No sooner had we turned her loose in the holding paddock than a big, white Arabian gelding came over to the fence to greet Annabelle. They touched noses. Shem was the only one, out of about a dozen nearby horses, to make an effort to welcome this new curly pony. It was a touching sight to see these two white horses meeting each other. They acted as though they were having a long-awaited reunion.

Painting, by the author, of
Shem greeting Annabelle

From day one, Annabelle adapted well. She was completely cooperative with Jane and never exhibited any of the bad behaviors we were warned about. In fact, within two days, Jane was riding her. I documented that process with my camera. It was a great process to watch. Jane's understanding of horses was both amazing and inspiring.

Within a year, Jane had Annabelle pulling a pony cart, giving rides to special-needs children. Jane's spiritual connection to Annabelle, via a long night of emotional dreams, turned out to be a real blessing for all of us.

Annabelle was unique in every way. Aside from the unusual curly hair, she had a unique way of "talking" to you. Typically, whenever she wanted something, usually just attention, she would stretch out her neck, look directly at you and then gently bob and shake her head.

One morning in particular, I saw for myself how tuned in to humans Annabelle was. I was doing my usual thing of getting her clean water while she was in a paddock. I grabbed an empty bucket, just one nearby, and filled it with fresh water. It might have been a blue or black bucket. I can't remember. In any case, Annabelle walked over to the water but wouldn't drink. Instead, she just put her nose over the bucket and kept shaking her head at me. I could tell by her stare that she wanted me to change something. I couldn't figure out what. Then I saw that we had a new orange bucket by the barn door. Just for fun, rather than out of any deep psychic awareness on my part, I poured her some fresh water in the spiffy orange bucket.

Wouldn't you know it? That rascal submerged nearly her whole head in this fancy new bucket and drank like a desert racehorse! From then on, she insisted on being served her H2O in her special chalice!

Annabelle was a great teacher. Her most apparent lesson taught me that we should never let anyone else's opinion about someone we haven't met eclipse our own intuition.

Horses connect spiritually first. Thankfully, Jane was open enough to hear the truth of this extraordinary animal's great soul. What if she hadn't trusted herself? Or honored the significance of the dream? This beautiful pony, with her unusual intelligence and special heart, might have been sold to a slaughterhouse.

I loved getting to know each of the 25 horses as individuals. Just like people, there are no two alike. The takeaway lesson here is, of course, we should never generalize. Not all men are anything… or all women… or all Republicans or Democrats… or all Phillies fans.

Every person…every animal is unique. Stereotypes are broken more often than not. Judging others, especially based on a secondhand opinion from someone else, is a guaranteed way to create a block to your own happiness.

Shem

One day I was busy cleaning the 10 stalls that lined the indoor riding arena. I assumed Jane was doing her thing on some other part of the farm. Suddenly I heard her extremely distressed voice yelling: "Get up, Shem! Get up! Please, Shem! You have to get up!"

I couldn't imagine what was going on. I ran into the riding arena. Jane was kicking, crying, pushing and obviously doing everything she could to coax a beautiful white Arabian horse, lying on its side, to get up. It was Shem, the noble white Arabian who had welcomed Annabelle to the farm. What a beautiful animal. I would later find out that he had been a gift, to Jane from her husband, some 18 years earlier.

"He has to get up!" Jane shouted as she looked at me pleadingly. "His insides are twisted! I know he's in pain! He's colicky! He's going to die if he doesn't get up! Please… help me get him up!"

I pulled on the lead rope as hard as I could, while Jane pushed, prodded and even kicked Shem from behind. Finally, but just barely, Shem came to his feet. His breathing was heavy. He was sweating profusely. Even I could tell he was a very sick horse.

Jane anxiously handed me the lead rope. "You have to make him walk, Tom. Just lead him around, while I go call the vet. Whatever you do, don't let him lie down!" She ran out of the barn.

There I was, suddenly in charge of an extremely stressed Arabian horse that wasn't familiar with me. All I knew about this horse was that he was in great pain and in danger of dying. My life and death instructions were to lead him around the arena and not let him lie down. I didn't have the time or luxury to be afraid.

So, as I always did when I was scared or lost, I turned everything over to God. How else was I going to get any help, any courage, and any healing power?

Somehow, I was able to get Shem to walk about a quarter of the way around the arena. All the while, it was evident that he desperately wanted to lie down. I didn't even know what colic was. But I understood that his life depended on me keeping him walking. His breathing was dramatically heavy. He was drenched in sweat. I felt so sorry for him. I just kept talking to him and coaxed him to take one feeble step after another. I did so as lovingly as I could. I knew I had to keep myself out of my own way, as I had done with Helen (Chapter 1) during her PTSD episode.

Without warning, Shem stopped. He stood as still as a statue. And I mean, honestly, it was as if he became a statue. His breathing returned to soft and regular. He even stopped sweating.

I didn't know what to think or do. I just stood there, under his noble head, looking at him. What happened next is not easy to explain. I'll do my best.

It's not like I felt stunned, or in any way shaken up, but I did suddenly feel that I was under Shem's "spell." That's when, in a split second (though it felt like about five minutes) Shem "downloaded" or, possibly, "transferred" all of his thoughts and feelings to me. Just as Cisco had done to Jane! I could hardly believe what happened.

What Shem transferred to me, however, about his life and indeed about his soul, didn't make me cry with sympathy because of a life of abuse. No. This noble statue made it clear that he'd had a blessed life and had always been treated with kindness.

What Shem gave me in that special moment of stillness, in the middle of an empty riding arena, was a most wonderful gift! It was the gift of taking something away. Something I never wanted to have. What noble Shem released me of — thankfully and amazingly — was all of my fear of horses! Somehow, at a spiritual level, Shem completely restored my confidence in the part of me that was born knowing, loving and trusting horses.

Wow! Stunned and amazed, I was filled with gratitude.

I don't know how else to describe what happened. When I looked into this magnificent animal's eyes, I knew the horse was telling me that my soul and the spirit of all horses were in complete harmony. He thanked me for being so loving. And he conveyed that he needed me to help his beloved Jane deal with his death.

All of that, in one magical moment, was conveyed, transferred and understood between Shem and me. My soul felt completely validated. I wasn't sure how to ever tell that story. But you just heard it.

Next, just as suddenly as he had stopped and stood so calm and still, Shem lowered his head and began heavy breathing again. Sweat started pouring out of his body. I gently coaxed him into walking. Only this time, I wasn't a tentative farmhand stressfully leading a strange horse, reluctant to move. No. This time we were two spirits, two soulmates walking together around a dusty riding arena, heart-to-heart committed to a singular mission. That mission, we both somehow understood, was to "Try Softly" enough to allow God's will to be done with assuredness, faith, and love.

Just then, Jane hastily re-entered the arena. "How is he? Has he been walking?" She came over and took the rope. "Come on, Shem," she gently invited, "Come on, buddy, let's walk. I'll sing to you."

And that's what we did. As we walked this beautiful white Arabian horse around the arena, Jane sang to him. Eighteen-year-old Shem struggled with every step. He kept throwing all of his weight to his hindquarters, trying to fall down. We managed to keep him up for another few steps. Then he went down. He rolled to his side. His breathing became loud and fast. He was practically drowning in sweat. I wondered how I would ever be able to tell Jane all that Shem had conveyed, especially the part about him being ready to die.

Jane and I both knelt to comfort the big, beautiful, sick white horse. We stroked his head and rubbed his neck. We spoke to him reassuringly. "The vet will be here soon." Jane let her tears flow down her cheeks. "Oh, Shem!" she cried, "I love you so much. Please hang on. Please! I know you can do it!"

As we knelt beside our downed friend, the late afternoon sun began to bathe the footing of the riding ring in soft light. "It's getting late. I hope the doctor gets here soon," Jane said.

All the while, I kept trying to figure out how best to tell her about my spiritual communication with Shem. I knew she would believe me and completely understand, as she lived like that all the time. Her communion with Cisco was a prime example. My only concern was about how to tell her that Shem was ready to transition.

For the time being, I decided to tell her everything, except the part about Shem asking me to help her accept his passing. That was the part I wanted to tell her the most, and the part she most needed to hear. But the time wasn't right. For all I knew, Dr. Coven would be able to help Shem recover. Maybe it wasn't colic after all.

I told Jane about my experience with Shem and how he joined his soul with mine and the souls of all horses. Of course, she understood. She knew me well enough by then to know that I was a good candidate to have such a spiritual experience with a horse. She also knew that Shem was the kind of noble soul to give such a gift.

"Shem is an amazing horse," she said. "He always looked out for me when I was riding him. As spirited as he is, and as much as he liked to dance around, if ever I would get off balance or start to come out of the saddle, he would put his body back under me. He always took care of me. He is a beautiful Spirit."

"I know," I said. "I just got a glimpse of his noble soul myself."

Dr. Coven arrived at the barn and rushed in with his medical bag. We filled him in on how Shem was doing. The seasoned vet readied himself to apply whatever treatment he could.

"The first thing we need to do is get him up," he said. "Let's see if we can do that." With immense effort, all three of us pulling and pushing, we finally got Shem back on his feet. Jane held his halter. I made sure to get myself out of the way.

Then Dr. Coven stood behind the horse and proceeded to insert his gloved hand to feel for internal blockage in his gut.

Suddenly, as if shot from a cannon, Shem's hind legs both blasted straight up! And he kicked Dr. Coven in the head! Oh my God!

As the elderly veterinarian stumbled backward, he clutched his face. He landed in a sitting position, in a cloud of dust, on the arena floor. He shook his head. I could see a slight red mark on his forehead. He managed to get up and brush himself off. He seemed to be ok.

Fortunately, being the experienced vet he was, the shaken horse doctor had been prepared for such a reaction. Thankfully, when the incident occurred, he had thrown his head back just far enough, and just in the nick of time, to avoid what could have been a lethal blow. All Shem's double-barreled kick was able to do was knock Dr. Coven's glasses off. Thank God!

I didn't say anything at the time, other than to make sure the doc was ok. But I knew what Shem was thinking. I knew that he just wanted to be left alone to die peacefully. I also knew that both he and Dr. Coven were doing their dance together for Jane's sake. No one was ready to tell her that Shem was not going to get better. Not me... not Dr. Coven... not even Shem. Not yet.

But I could see Dr. Coven was doing his best to lay the groundwork for such sad news. He told Jane directly that it looked like Shem's insides were very likely twisted and blocking his digestion. We all could see that the ailing horse was in pain. She understood what was taking place. Naturally, she wanted to give Shem every chance to survive. When she asked Dr. Coven if there was any possibility of Shem's recovery, he said there is always a possibility, provided Shem would drink some water and be able to move his bowels. But he was quite honest about saying that Shem's chances were very slim.

Dr. Coven agreed to come back later and check on Shem's progress. He gave the poor horse something to help with the pain.

Shem lay down, obviously in pain, when Dr. Coven left. That's when Kay came into the arena. She joined us in a prayer vigil. The three of us spontaneously stood around the downed Arabian. We held hands and said prayers aloud for his recovery.

Dr. Coven returned a few hours later. Shem seemed pretty much the same. Jane decided she was going to gather some blankets and sleep beside Shem all night. Dr. Coven said he would come back tomorrow. Before he left, he handed Jane medications to help with Shem's pain. Kay and I stayed till dark. Upon leaving, we told Jane to call us if she needed anything. Jane prepared for an all-night vigil with her beloved Shem.

The next morning, after a restless night of worrying about Jane and her dying horse, I couldn't stay away any longer. I got up, dressed, and was at the barn by 6:00 a.m. Nobody had called me; I just had to be there.

When I walked into the arena, I was surprised to see Shem standing! Not only that, Jane was brushing him. The big Arabian looked as if he was on the road to recovery. I felt silly for being so sure of myself that he was ready to die. But I was glad to be wrong. Kay arrived soon after me.

Just as the three of us were talking about the "miracle" of how Shem seemed to be recovering, the noble animal collapsed to the ground. By the time Dr. Coven got there about 9:00, Shem was in terrible pain. We all could see it. The doctor tried everything he could. Then he told Jane that he was afraid it was going to be a losing battle. Because he knew her so well, including how much this particular horse meant to her, he just couldn't bring himself to tell her "for sure" that Shem wasn't going to bounce back. But he knew it. We all did. Just as we all knew it would have to be Jane's call.

"Can't we give it two more hours, please?" Jane pleaded.

"Sure," Doctor Coven said. "I'll be back before noon." He walked out of the arena.

"I need to go make a phone call," Kay said. "I'll be back in a few minutes."

Jane, Shem and I were alone in the arena. She was cradling Shem's head on her lap. I was on the other side of the horse, kneeling. I tried to comfort both of them. Then Shem did something so unusual that Jane still talks about it to this day. And remember, she was a horsewoman with over 40 years of experience around hundreds of horses. The dying horse—my spiritual soulmate on some unexplainable level—suddenly stopped his heavy breathing. Once again, with complete calm and composure, Shem slowly lifted his neck almost straight up. Then, very slowly and deliberately, the downed Arabian turned his head toward me. "Oh my God!" Jane exclaimed.

"Tom, he's looking right at you! Oh my God! I've never seen a horse act like this! What is he saying?"

It was such a profoundly moving moment and experience for all of us. There is no way I can tell this story without tears springing to my eyes. I knew exactly what Shem was saying. As, by now, I'm sure you do too.

I looked at Jane. "Do you want to know what he's saying?"

She nodded through her tears.

"He is saying that he was noble all his life. Now he is asking you to do the noble thing and release him to continue on his spiritual journey. He wants you to let him die."

There... I'd finally said it... The Truth. How did Jane handle it? She thanked me first then kissed Shem, then jumped up and ran out of the barn to catch the vet.

Thanks to Kay having a conversation with Dr. Coven, he was still on the property. Right away, he came back into the riding arena with the needle he needed to relieve Shem of his suffering. Kay, Jane, Dr. Coven and I offered silent prayers to the beautiful Shem, as his soul lifted unto Heaven.

Mother's Nature

The day after Shem's passing, Jane needed to take a solo ride on Cisco. She wanted to be by herself after the painful passing of her beloved Arabian friend. While she was on her ride, her cellphone rang. It was her mother. Jane was surprised to hear from her at that time of the day. The conversation began with her mom saying: "Hi, honey. I hope you don't think I'm crazy, but I had a visitation last night."

"What do you mean, Mom?" Jane asked. She'd already told her mom that she had to put Shem down. But she hadn't shared anything about how he died.

"Well, I'll just read you what I wrote. I wrote it all down. I have it right here. And as I was writing this, I could see you riding Shem across a lovely field, his mane and tail flowing, and I could feel the wind as you rode by. Here's what I wrote:

"I awoke around 4:00 a.m. and was very restless. I could not go to sleep. I was in and out of bed. I felt anxious about something. After struggling for a while, I started to pray in the Spirit. Then I felt a strong presence of Shem. He was letting me know that Jane should no longer grieve for him, for he was at peace. He had been in pain for quite some time. Shem tried to stay because he did not want to leave her. He was in so much pain, he finally had to let go. His bowels and insides were so twisted. He no longer wanted to suffer. Now Annabelle will love Jane just as much as Shem did. He died to find peace. I relaxed and cuddled against Daddy and fell asleep."

"Wow! Thank you, Mom. Thank you for validating what I feel about Shem and Annabelle. You're the opposite of crazy! I'm out riding now, on Cisco. I've been trying to put Shem's death in perspective. You called at the perfect time. Thank you, Mom. I love you. Everything you just said is reassuring and comforting. You just helped me a lot. You and Shem."

Through her tears, Jane managed to tell her dear mother goodbye. "Thanks again, Mom, I'll call you later." She gently urged Cisco into a trot.

I know it's part of life—the deepest, richest realm of pure love and spirituality—because I live in that open territory as well, and yet I am still always amazed by these wonderful happenings. When you are open enough, all barriers of separation dissolve. Life becomes an awe-inspiring dance of faith, truth, and love. Spiritual communication begins to flow like water, especially to those who are "Trying Softly" enough to be open to the Spirit of the horse.

From my earliest childhood and the days of my cowgirl heroine Sally Starr, horses have been my spiritual teachers. The only regret I ever had about those wonderful childhood days was that I had never properly thanked Sally Starr for giving me my pony. Of course, I thanked her that day on her TV show, as a little boy. But later in life, after putting the significance of that pony-winning experience in perspective, and even writing a book about it (MEMO), I wasn't able to thank her the way I wanted to, before she died.

Jane and pretty much all others who had read my book assured me that Sally knew how much Lucky meant to me. I'm sure she did. And I know that making my dream come true warmed her heart. I only wish I could have gotten my book to her on time. I feel all the time that my angel cowgirl is always watching over me and all of these horse experiences. Though it was six decades earlier, I can still see her beautiful smile.

From Shakespeare's Henry V: "When I bestride him, I soar, I am a hawk: He trots the air: The earth sings when he touches it: the basest horn of his hoof is more musical than the pipes of Hermes."

Chapter 20

Full Circle – Full Bloom

"Trying Softer" means trusting the Universe to bring you Home to your Heart.

I loved volunteering at the horse farm every day. Thanks to Shem's mysterious cleansing, I had released all fear of horses. Being able to relax around the horses enhanced both my ability and enjoyment when it came to helping Jane with the necessary chores. How freeing! I even learned a little about horse training.

Being around the horses had become my life. I went to the farm every morning. Typically, I put in a good eight-hour day. If not doing something with my kids or grandkids, I made myself available for weekend work when needed. After about a year, I'd learned enough about farm work that Jane and her husband even trusted me to be in charge of things when they went on vacations.

After what was always a fulfilling day with the animals, I usually came home to my apartment feeling tired. But it was that good kind of tired, the kind that comes from doing physical work you love. My evenings then would generally be spent painting, writing or perhaps sharing time with Judy.

After a while, Judy and I started casually dating. Neither of us tried to steer the relationship in any direction. We shared a deep soul connection and always gave each other plenty of space.

As we worked around the farm together, Jane and I shared many conversations. One of my favorite things to talk about was Judy. I was so smitten with Judy at the time, I couldn't help it. Jane fully understood. She had met Judy and really liked her. She was happy for both of us. I even went to Jane for dating advice.

I recall one time in particular when Jane went beyond the call of duty to help me prepare a surprise picnic for Judy. We were doing wheelbarrow trips back and forth from the sawdust pile. I casually mentioned that I wanted to surprise Judy with a little picnic supper after she got off work. Jane parked her wheelbarrow. "I'll be right back!" she called over her shoulder as she rushed into the farmhouse. I had no idea what she was doing. I just continued making soft beds for the horses. About 15 minutes later, Jane returned carrying a perfect little picnic basket, filled with goodies, including flowers and a bottle of wine.

"This is what you need."

Being around such good-hearted folks as Jane's family and all of their wonderful rescued animals brought me healing. The people, the horses, the whole environment helped me grow, expand and become more of myself every day. Concerning "Trying Softer," the whole new lifestyle—including the regular physical labor—enabled me to release any residual blocks I might have been harboring to becoming happier and healthier. All the while, Judy's love kept my heart alive with hope for a future with my soulmate.

Photo of me on Delilah

A Big Surprise

One day, Jane surprised me with an incredible gift. It was the gift of a horse of my own! She said it was her way of thanking me for all of my volunteer work. I was moved to tears. My horse's name was Delilah. She was a buckskin

Missouri Fox Trotter. She looked like "Buttermilk," the horse always ridden by Roy Roger's wife, Dale Evans.

Delilah was beautiful. Standing almost sixteen hands tall, she had an easy disposition. Both her mane and tail were black, long and flowing. We bonded instantly. Soon Delilah and I were going on trail rides with Jane and other friends who boarded their horses at the farm.

Both Jane and her husband are good-hearted and successful people. Likewise, their children have grown into adulthood doing very well. Their son Louie is one most notable. His commitment and contribution to helping special-needs children and their families are inspirational to me and loads of others.

Leg Up Farm

It all began when Louie and his wife gave birth to a special-needs daughter. From then on, Louie made it his life's mission to obtain the best treatment in the world for his little girl. That heart-centered quest to help their daughter eventually led Louie to establish a state-of-the-art therapy center in his own community. It sits on 18 acres of donated land. He named it Leg Up Farm.

Leg Up Farm is the non-profit organization founded by Louie, otherwise known as Louis J. Castriota Jr. The mission of Leg Up Farm is to enrich the lives of individuals with special needs and their families, through support and customized programs. They are the only facility in the country to provide physical, occupational, aquatic, equine and speech therapy, in addition to counseling and nutritional services, educational and recreational programming, and a variety of equine-assisted activities — all under one roof. Typically, in any given year, Louie's amazing treatment center provides upwards of 20,000 therapy appointments.

Establishing such a beautiful and effective therapy center has enabled Louie to help thousands of other children and families, as well as his own daughter. As of this writing, since opening in 2010 Leg Up Farm has served over 2,000 children and their families.

Louie even wrote an inspiring book about his life. It's the story of how he realized his dream to help thousands of children. His book is titled: LEG UP, *The Courage to Dream.* Visit www.LegUpFarm.org to learn more. Donations are always needed and greatly appreciated.

Louie's story is heroic. The obstacles he faced in the process of making his dream come true were incredibly daunting. How he overcame them is nothing short of amazing. Eventually, thanks to his total faith and unwavering persistence, Louie won the hearts of enough people around the country, as well as in the community, to support this non-profit venture and blessing.

Along his heart-path, as his book reveals—after so many ups and downs—Louie ultimately found the "Try Softer" balance that allows for success. Today, he continues to expand therapeutic services throughout our community to include helping special-needs adults.

I had never met Louie until a few months after I started helping at his parents' farm. One day as we finished stall cleaning, Jane asked me if I would like to visit Leg Up Farm and meet her son Louie. I welcomed the opportunity. I had heard of Leg Up Farm but didn't even know where it was located. Based on its reputation, however, I knew it would be a place that would touch my heart. I thought to myself (which turned out to be exactly right) If Leg Up Farm was a place to help special-needs children (remember my little friend, Flipper)... if it was a place of counseling and therapy (very appealing to the therapist in me)... and if it had horses for equine therapy, then wow and Holy Cow! How could it not be my idea of Heaven!

Eager to meet Louie and get a tour of the facility, I took along a copy of my book, *MEMO From Your Soul,* to see if he would trade me for a copy of his own book.

After setting up an appointment, Jane drove us to Leg Up Farm. Louie greeted us at the main desk. From the beginning, her son was gracious and kind. He seemed just as pleased to give us a tour as we were to experience it. The tour group that day consisted of Jane, another woman she had gone to high school with, and me. Her school friend was interested in perhaps volunteering at the facility.

As we walked around the beautiful campus, I felt quite moved. Seeing the kids in their classrooms and working at their therapy stations overwhelmed me. I was tearfully reminded of my days many years earlier when working with "Flipper" and other children at the Child Development Center. Back then, I was always frustrated because of overcrowding and lack of resources. On this day, in addition to seeing how caring and competent the staff of Leg Up Farm was, my heart practically exploded with joy in the presence of every imaginable therapeutic resource.

I loved everything about the place: the location, the state-of-the-art layout, the modern facilities, indoor and out— including the largest therapeutic Koi pond in the country— the fantastic playground (built by a thousand volunteers in one week) and the huge barn with its indoor riding arena and observation deck. The loving atmosphere was palpable.

After the tour, Louie and I exchanged books. I shared with him how much I loved his facility. My heart was especially moved by his mission of helping not only the identified special-needs children but also their siblings and parents as well. I told him that I was eager to support Leg Up Farm, in any way I could.

One way I thought I might be able to help was by donating paintings. So that's what I did whenever a fundraising event came up. If you visit my website: www.sageandbrush.com

and click on the tab at the top that says: Leg Up Farm, you can see the kinds of paintings I have done to help the center raise money. I continue to set aside paintings for the next fundraising auction.

Right Place-Right Time

So many avenues of synchronicity had led me along my path: From my pony... to my counseling of children... to my becoming an artist... and now to meeting a family that brought together everything I loved, including giving me my own horse! I could hardly believe my blessings. All of that plus connecting with my soulmate Judy! I couldn't help but feel that having all of this come together in the autumn of my life, in one place... I must have done SOMETHING right along my journey. I must have "tried softly" enough—enough of the time—to remain unblocked enough to receive so many blessings.

Judy's Niche

In addition to the large therapy center and school for special-needs children, Louie also established a wonderful whole-food grocery store. He called it Leg Up Farmer's Market. It was a newly constructed store located only a few miles from the therapy center. Louie's purpose and mission in establishing the market were to provide the healthiest food and nutritional supplements he could find to health-conscious folks in our area. It was yet another manifestation of Louie's wanting to improve the lives of others.

Around that same time, Judy started to burn out from her job at the fitness center. Among many other talents, she had years of training as a nutritionist and all-around health expert. She was frustrated at her job at the fitness center because of not being able to share her natural gifts and talents. Instead, most of her day-to-day responsibilities had to do with cleaning the place and selling memberships. The real Judy knew she had a lot more to contribute. Her grieving over Chris's death had obviously taken her to deeper realms of her own personhood. Though I was sad about the way it happened, it warmed my heart to see how open Judy had become to accepting all of her feelings.

There was nothing Judy cared more about than helping others grow into happier and healthier individuals, young or old. She loved all people, especially children. She'd even had her own state-approved daycare center in the past. She was a whole person with a natural passion for all things healthy.

When I shared with Judy the story of Leg Up Farm, and how its mission was so loving and inspired, her face lit up like a shining star. We excited each other as we talked about how she might fit in with such a wonderful cause. I did my part to encourage her to put in an application.

One thing led to another, and the opportunity finally came for Judy to leave her job at the fitness center to work at the Leg Up Farmer's Market. She was thrilled to be hired. And a perfect fit for the job. Not only was she the perfect resource to help the customers select the foods and nutritional supplements best for them, she was also finally able to make a difference in people's health by sharing her knowledge. The more Judy was able to help others, the better she began to feel. She was a "natural" at allowing the "Try Softer" way to heal her heart. The only problem was, at first, Judy's job at the market was part-time. That was because the store was still getting up and running. But that put Judy in a financial bind. She needed to earn more money to pay her rent.

Well, as non-coincidences have it, another part-time receptionist's position JUST HAPPENED to open at the Leg Up Farm Therapy center. She filled out an application and was immediately hired to work at the front desk. Perfect timing!

Everyone at Leg Up Farm, especially the families who came there for therapy appointments, immediately welcomed her. She shared with me how rewarding her new position was, and how much she enjoyed getting to know the children and their families. Finally, in her new role, Judy was able to be her true self and share even more of her gifts and abilities. She felt freer to no longer have to cope with such an unrewarding position at the fitness center. Now she could fly with Leg Up Farm. They even asked her to do drum circles on a regular basis, an activity she gladly performed without pay just to help the Leg Up mission. On occasion, I joined in to help Judy with the drumming.

It is an understatement to say that Leg Up Farm is a vital asset to the York, Pennsylvania, area. You can't visit either the therapy center or the market without feeling the love. I am thankful that the entire community has embraced Leg Up Farm and continues to support all of their services with much-needed donations.

Then it Happened—the Full Circle Coincidence

One spring morning, I was at the horse farm doing my usual chores. I had just brought up three bales of hay, by wheelbarrow, along the main road, to toss out to a small herd of rescued ponies. I was in the process of throwing hay over the fence when I heard Jane running up the road toward me. I hadn't seen her for a couple of days. She was very excited.

"OK," she said, trying to catch her breath, "I have something to tell you that you're going to love. But I need to give you a little background first. Take a seat on that bale of hay, and listen to everything I'm going to say. This is amazing!"

I sat on one of the bales. I was all ears.

Jane: "To begin, as I think you know, my son Louie worked in the broadcast industry as a sales manager for over 20 years. For the last 14 of those years, even while selling advertising, he also managed to build Leg Up Farm. In 2010, he left TV to become President and CEO of Leg Up Farm. In 2012, Louie received an award called the 'Lew and Janet Klein Award.' It's a very prestigious award for broadcasters making a significant difference in the lives of others. Are you with me so far?"

"Yep, I'm following every word."

Jane continued: "OK. At that ceremony for Louie, I had the honor of meeting Mr. H. Lewis Klein. He was in attendance at the awards ceremony, but, unfortunately, his wife Janet wasn't able to be there due to an injury she had sustained from a fall. Mr. Klein is very well-known and respected. Some have given him the nickname of 'Mr. Philadelphia.' He's quite famous in the world of television. I met him briefly, just long enough to thank him for honoring my son. He actually discovered Dick Clark! Now here comes the part you are going to love. Is this interesting yet?"

"Are you kidding? I'm on the edge of my bale." I could feel my excitement growing.

Jane continued: "Last night, at the annual meeting of the Pennsylvania Association of Broadcasters at the Hershey Hotel, the opposite thing happened. This time we were there for my husband to receive special recognition for his numerous contributions to the broadcasting industry. And during the evening, I got to meet Mrs. Klein. And during our conversation, I asked if her husband ever worked at WFIL TV in Philly. Because I know that's where you won your pony. She said he did, and that he produced 'Bandstand.'"

"Wait a minute!" I interrupted. "Are you going to tell me that he knew Sally Starr?"

Jane: "Now wait... not only did he know her, Mr. Klein also produced her show! He enabled Sally Starr to be all that she was!"

"Wow! I can't believe this coincidence! Did you tell Mrs. Klein about me, and that I won a pony on his (Sally's) show?"

Jane: "Yes. I didn't have a chance to talk to Mr. Klein this time, but I did tell his wife Janet that you are helping us on the farm... and that you wrote a book called *MEMO From Your Soul* that tells the whole Sally Starr story. And guess what she said! She said that it would be wonderful for her husband to meet you and read your book! I'm sure they are both intrigued by your life and how they influenced your path.

"Isn't this amazing?" Jane exclaimed. "How can these things happen!?"

"Yeah, it is really amazing! This is an impossible coincidence!" I could not hide my joy. "You're right," I said with goosebumps breaking out, "I love hearing this!"

Jane smiled. "I couldn't wait to tell you."

"I'm definitely going to send the Kleins a copy of my book," I said. "I need to write a letter explaining how much they helped shape my life. I have to tell them how having my fondest dream come true, thanks to them and Sally, prepared me to stay on my own heart-path all these years. A path that now brings me back to them. I feel so grateful to them! I hope I can put my feelings into words. I need some time to digest this one," I said, laughing with joy.

"Now I'll be able to thank Sally this way! I think I told you she died before I could get a copy of my book to her. But now, thanks to you — and the accomplishments of your husband and son — I can thank the man who gave Sally her career. Man... this is beyond coincidence! I can't believe it! Wow. Thank you, Jane." I gave her a big hug.

Deep Gratitude

I left the farm early that day, eager to get home and write a letter to the Kleins. I couldn't have been more excited. It was almost as if Lucky had somehow come back to me. Or brought me back to myself! Or something! Not that she'd ever "left," certainly not from my heart. I had even secretly thought in some spiritual way that maybe Delilah was Lucky, reincarnated. That was the kind of feeling I had upon first meeting her. And now who should re-enter my life but the same man who gave me Lucky. The same man who enabled Sally Star to become the unforgettable cowgirl host of a TV show that had a positive influence in the lives of thousands of children! The spiritual significance of these occurrences continued to exhilarate me!

This sequence of full-circle events spanning half a century was no coincidence, no kind of happenstance. No, this was clearly God's orchestration. How else could such a fortuitous and soulful reunion have been coordinated?

I wrote Mr. H. Lewis Klein a long letter from my heart. It was essentially a letter of gratitude. I didn't keep a copy, but I remember describing myself as a kind of seed that he had planted, back in 1957. Noting that I was but one of the thousands of seeds that he sowed, (perhaps millions) simply by being himself and producing Sally Starr's great show. I used the metaphor of how that seed, like so many others he planted, had grown and blossomed into a flower that had now returned to him. Along with the letter, I also sent Mr. Klein a copy of my book.

Within a week of receiving my book and my letter, Mr. Philadelphia kindly responded with a handwritten note:

Dear Thomas,

Having read MEMO FROM YOUR SOUL and your beautiful letter, I feel as though we have had a longtime friendship. Your thoughts are an inspiring message to me. Once I began to read your book, I couldn't put it down. MEMO FROM YOUR SOUL was so meaningful and relevant for me. Although I haven't seen your watercolors, I know they must have been painted with wisdom and passion. You have shown so many people they too have a pony to achieve. I hope someday we meet again. It would be a privilege. The love you express, I am sure, is a reflection of the love so many have of you. Tom, you are a blessing.

Warmly, Lew.

Soon after receiving that beautiful letter from Mr. Klein, I received a second letter from him and his wife. That letter was an invitation for me to visit them at their home. My farm owner friends were invited also. Jane's husband graciously offered to do the driving. I happily seized this fantastic opportunity and made the necessary arrangements to travel to their home for an afternoon visit. It was a day I will never forget. I felt both humbled and honored to be able to spend some time with a couple who, simply by being themselves and living a heart-centered life, profoundly changed my life.

Upon meeting Mr. Klein, I instantly felt that our soulful connection bonded both of us. Through my own tears, I could see his eyes watering as we first shook hands. Seeing that both he and Janet were in excellent health warmed my heart. I could tell they were doing well, living on their own in their long-time home.

After a brief inside tour, we took a lovely backyard garden walk. Then we had a delicious lunch. When we were finished, I snuck out to the car and brought in a surprise gift painting I had created for them. They accepted my gift with as much graciousness as gratitude.

While sitting on the Kleins' back patio enjoying wonderful conversation, I could feel Sally Starr's spirit with us. The whole afternoon felt not only like a profoundly spiritual reunion for me, but a significant renewal of my soul. That naively confident, determined and faithful 10-year-old pony-winning boy was alive and well. The Lightning-T-Horseshoe had struck again!

During our visit, Mr. Klein confirmed all of my most positive thoughts about Sally Starr. He verified what a truly wonderful woman she was. From that day on, the Kleins and I became very close friends. I love them both.

Journey to the Heart

My deepest sense of self was validated when I was 10. Finding my pony did it for me. I was a confirmed man of faith from that moment on. As I've continued my journey into adulthood and now entering old age, I've always tried (admittedly sometimes too hard) to maintain my authenticity. I believe that following my heart, marching to the beat of my own drummer, all the while knowing when to get out of my own way, are keys that have enabled me to realize my fondest dreams.

Clearly, the arc of my life has always bent toward love. It's amazing to me how, all along the way but particularly in these last chapters of my life, I've been continuously reunited not only with deeper parts of my most authentic self, but also with the key spiritual collaborators who started me on my heart-path, and/or kept me going in the "right" direction in the first place.

Of all the "coincidences" in my life, many of which you now know about, I think the most mind-blowing of all was reconnecting with H. Lewis Klein. Here's why:

As you've already learned, I was born loving horses. When I won my pony on the Sally Starr show at age 10, my core being was completely validated. I don't know how else to say it. I wasn't just a happy kid who "luckily" won a pony. I was a happy kid who knew he was forever securely connected to the Universe, God, Life, and Love, and that his soul would never let him down.

The experience of having my fondest dream come true would have been wonderful enough. But the experience of having my fondest dream come true WHILE CONSCIOUSLY SEEING AND UNDERSTANDING my part in the manifestation process is almost too incredible to describe.

Because of my "peak experience" at such a formative age, I became a person of absolute faith. I relied on that faith at every critical decision-making point in my life. Each time I had to jump off a cliff to land more into myself, that faith was God's hand holding me up. After being so aligned—Body/Mind/Spirit—with the Universe, how could I ever deny that we are all part of God?

Since my pony experience, I've always felt that Sally Starr was my Spiritual Godmother. I didn't necessarily tell anybody that. Nor, in those early days, did I even try to contact Sally to thank her. It was only later in my life, after realizing what a profound impact she'd had, that I attempted to reach out to her. Unfortunately, as I mentioned earlier, by then it was too late.

Sadly, Sally Starr passed before I could get a copy of my book — *MEMO FROM YOUR SOUL* — to her. As so much of the book is a detailed description of my pony story, I'm sure she would have loved it. The more I realized how my "Lightning-T-Horseshoe"-confirmed faith helped me to reach so many goals, the more gratitude I felt. I always thanked "Our Gal Sal" silently in my prayers. I credited her for helping me have the courage to jump off the cliff with Watercolor Wings and commit to realizing the artist within, without even knowing how to paint. Just as I knew I was going to win my pony when I was 10, later, as an adult on a new mission, I knew I was going to become an artist. That knowing — that trusting myself — led me to meeting a banker who was willing to pay me for as many paintings as I wanted to do, as much as I wanted to charge.

I credited Sally and my pony experience for enabling me to have enough trust in the Universe to leave an unhealthy marriage and follow the knock-knock-knocking on the door of my heart. That choice led me to my nine-hour, tearful, cathartic breakthrough... which led me to my soulmate, Judy... which led me to meeting my kind friends, Jane and her husband... which enabled me to reconnect with the original love of my life (that had set my soul on fire in the first place)... horses. All of that caused my whole family to celebrate with a huge sigh of relief to see that I was finally becoming so much of myself that I could not contain my joy. My children, Ben and Amanda, especially were very happy to see their dad finally in a loving relationship, not only with Judy... but with himself too.

Finally, thanks to an incredible series of synchronicities, I was given the opportunity to go even deeper behind the scenes and actually thank the man who gave Sally the opportunity to be all that she was.

The non-coincidence of the whole Sally Starr episode of my life coming back to me, after six decades, validated my life's journey. I hadn't just been randomly moving through my experiences like a ball being batted around in a pinball machine. I had, obviously and oh so thankfully, always been on a spiraling journey—with each experience moving closer to my heart and to my most authentic self.

Ultimately, after we finally stop blocking it, we are all headed "home" to our hearts. Coming home requires only a matter of accepting it.

Your life can be just as rewarding. The first thing you need to do is to let go of all of the outside distractions, diversions, and noise always trying to get you to do this, do that... be this, be that. Let the outside world have all of its noise and frenzy. It doesn't have to concern you. You'll need to get quiet and get reacquainted with yourself.

To find your own way home to your heart, stop trying so hard to please others. You'll need to allow all good things to flow into your world. No more blocking everything from fear. It's never too late to reconnect with the Universe, God, Life, and Love. Hey... if hearts can drop out of the sky—as they did for me—as gifts of loving support from deceased loved ones, then anything is possible.

My story is not special. It's just my journey. Your story is every bit as interesting and inspiring. And it is as perfect for you as my path is for me. The key is to be open. Open to all that is.

Be grateful for the "coincidences" in your life. Understand that they are helpful signs and signals reassuring you that you are still on your heart-path. Be thankful to God every morning you rise that you're granted another day in this wondrous world.

My Deepest Motivation

If I were asked to identify the single, bottom-line, most soulfully rooted thing that has inspired me to stay on the path that I feel I was born to follow—in spite of all kinds of challenges, pressures, and temptations—it would be: MY LOVE FOR MY CHILDREN AND GRANDCHILDREN. From my soul, I've always felt an unwavering commitment to not just TELL them but SHOW them this truth: In this lifetime—the one you create with your choices and perceptions—if you keep the faith, trust your heart, stay open and respectful to the wisdom of God's whispers:

There is no dream you can't realize.

I'm a very happy person; certainly, I am blessed beyond what I can even begin to fathom. I have the greatest family and friends in the world, and happiness is what I've always felt I owed all of my loved ones. I consciously choose to offer my happiness as a tribute to who they are, as the fullest expression of my heart. What better gift can I share than being my real, whole, happy and fulfilled self?

My greatest wish for my kids and grandkids is for them to walk with honesty, respect, and love on their own heart-paths, with unshakable faith, that, no matter what, if they don't block it they can win all the ponies they long for.

"Try Softer" is indeed a healthy formula for happiness. It is a way—perhaps even the ONLY way (because it is so much about balance)—for you to create a life where frustration, depression, anxiety, and disillusionment are replaced by contentment, happiness, relaxation and confirmed faith. It is the path of least resistance.

Yet it is not a strategy for avoiding pain. Even if you follow your most authentic self, and stay committed entirely to your heart-path, you will still need to face your fears, feel your pain, and suffer through many struggles. (Remember my dream of being chased around that little white house, and how I finally turned to face my fears?) It's a good thing, and a healthy truth, that we need to face the negatives in our lives and deal with them, as well as the positives.

God has certainly given us plenty of contrast and diversity to learn from. We can't appreciate resting until we make ourselves tired. We can't appreciate happiness until we know the depths of sadness. Nor can we know clarity without first feeling confused. And we will never find ourselves until we are lost. The truth is: pain is essential to our growth. And depending on how much of ourselves we want to discover, develop, experience and share, we will have to climb some very steep personal-growth mountains.

One of the hardest things to do in life is to allow our loved ones to have their struggles. Naturally, we want to do everything we can to help them out and eliminate their pain. In many instances that is what we can and should do. Any time and any way we can help someone, we should. It is kind and considerate to do everything we can to make life easier for those we care about. The truth is, however, we can go too far in our efforts to make life easier for another. Sometimes, the most compassionate thing we can do is allow another person to "have" their situation, circumstances, and struggle. Even their pain. Sometimes a little "tough love" is the greatest gift you can give someone.

It was difficult for me to do, but finally very helpful for me to learn how to accept other people's pain and struggles. I'm sure that made it easier for me to face my own challenges. Discomfort is our way of telling ourselves not only that something is wrong, but also that we have an opportunity to heal a part of ourselves that needs more love.

If you feel that some things in your life are wrong and painful and you would like to change them, consider doing so in an honest, self-accepting and God-trusting way. Consider the "Try Softer" way. Remember: it is a generous person—not a selfish person—who takes care of themselves first so that they can be optimally prepared to serve others.

If you try too hard to bypass the process of growth and development, even when your motives are good, your efforts will become increasingly counterproductive. You are better off to recognize and meet each challenge as it presents itself along your journey. The best way to do that is to keep both eyes on the path, in the present.

I couldn't find who wrote it, but the following parable teaches what I am trying to say. It also speaks to the heart of the message the master was trying to tell the Japanese boy at the beginning of this book:

The Story of the Butterfly

A man found a cocoon of a butterfly. One day a small opening appeared. He sat and watched the butterfly for several hours as it struggled to squeeze its body through the tiny hole. Then it stopped as if it couldn't go further.

The man decided to help the butterfly. He took a pair of scissors and snipped off the remaining bits of cocoon. The butterfly emerged easily, but it had a swollen body and shriveled wings.

The man continued to watch it, expecting that any minute the wings would enlarge and expand enough to support the body. Neither happened!

In fact, the butterfly spent the rest of its life crawling around. It was never able to fly.

What the man in his kindness and haste did not understand: The restricting cocoon and the struggle required by the butterfly to get through the opening was a way of forcing the fluid from the body into the wings so that it would be ready for flight once that was achieved.

Sometimes struggles are precisely needed in our lives. Going through life with no obstacles would cripple us. We would not be as strong as we could have been and we would never fly.

Stop over-analyzing. Life is simple. All emotions are beautiful.

When you eat, appreciate every last bite. Open your mind, arms, and heart to new things and people; we are united in our differences.

Ask the next person you see what their passion is, and share your inspiring dream with them. Travel often; getting lost will help you find yourself.

Some opportunities come only once. Seize them. Life is about the people you meet and the things you create with them, so go out and start creating.

Life is short.

Live your dream and wear your passion.

"I hope you don't think, Doc, just because I'm overanxious, overworked, overweight, overextended, overwrought, overtired, over the hill, and over any hope of getting better, that you have to over-charge me."

Busy as a Beaver

I was working in a factory during my first summer out of high school. "Beaver," how he introduced himself, was built like a fireplug with a firecracker personality to match. He had a black, perfectly cropped flat top and a round baby face. I don't think I ever saw him not smiling. Everybody liked him. His eyes always looked as if he was on the verge of pulling some kind of prank, which he generally did a few times each day.

I think he'd been working at the plant for about 25 years. Though he complained a lot, you could tell Beaver liked his job. At least you could tell he enjoyed the camaraderie and the daily joking around. In spite of how well he fit in, everyone knew that Beaver's constant obsession was to retire as soon as possible.

He used to brag that he had a *system* to beat the system. His master plan to retire sooner rather than later was simply to double shift. He said he was willing to temporarily sacrifice spending time with his family to bring in some fat paychecks. He wasn't sure how long he could do it, but Beaver's plan was to put not only his nose but his whole body and being to the grindstone and push himself as hard as necessary to build up a good retirement cushion. "I'll do anything for my kids, man," he'd say. And you could tell from the emotion in his voice and teary eyes that he meant it.

Beaver was full of energy. Therefore, every time he would broadcast his mantra about how "double shifting" was going to enable him to have "The Life of Riley" when he retired, I thought to myself: I guess if anybody can do it, Beaver can. In the back of my mind, I figured he'd last maybe a couple of months. How anybody could work 16 or more hours a day at that kind of hard work, I couldn't imagine. But Beaver was unique, to say the least. Because this was during the time of the Viet Nam war, and all of our jobs had to do with making military equipment, the company was more than willing to give everybody extra hours.

A couple of weeks before I left for college, Beaver finally, and confidently, put his plan of "sprinting to the finish line" into full gear. During my last days on the job, I watched with both amazement and curiosity as my eager Beaver friend clocked out with us every day, and then clocked back in to begin another shift. His attitude was clearly: "Hey, I'm rockin' this, man!" As I said, he was a "firecracker!"

I joined the Air Force and pretty much forgot about Beaver. It wasn't until several years after I got out of the service that I ran into a guy that used to work with us. At that moment, a delightful mental picture of Mr. Howell from Gilligan's Island popped into my head. "Hey, what happened to our friend Beaver?" I asked. "Is he living the Life of Riley on some island?"

"Didn't you hear?" my friend replied, looking down. "Beaver died of a massive heart attack the day before he was to retire."

Stanley Beaverson was survived by his wife and three young children.

Quiet Strength

A couple of weeks ago I met a woman named Christine Miller. She happened to be seated next to me in a restaurant. In my head, I was still writing this book and musing about my "Try Softer" thesis. Even though I was lost in thought, trying to figure out how to organize a good first draft, I was open to acknowledging the people around me.

I noticed that the couple sitting next to me seemed very relaxed. Their energy was good. They appeared retired. Other than their calm demeanor, nothing particularly notable about either of them showed up. They just looked like regular, friendly folks.

After striking up a casual conversation, I learned that Christine was a retired elementary school teacher. Further conversation revealed the following story:

Christine shared that she loved children and had always wanted to become a teacher. She said it wasn't easy and that she had to overcome many obstacles, including personal, financial and situational, but eventually, she enrolled in college at the age of 40.

She and her husband were caring people of faith who loved participating in various kinds of fundraisers. They regularly went out of their way to help those less fortunate. Even while she was in college, rearing a daughter and helping her husband manage their small farm, Christine volunteered to work with at-risk inner-city youth.

One day, just after graduating from college and getting her teaching certificate, she was in a low-income section of Baltimore, known as "the Projects." She was trying to help a mother with her two chronically truant sons. She stepped outside of the apartment for a minute, to take a break. Looking up at the sky, she felt suddenly inspired to ask God to tell her where she was meant to teach.

Christine: "God told me to look straight ahead. There was an elementary school about a block and a half away. It literally was right there in front of my eyes! And God said: 'That is where you will be teaching." Then I said to God: "So that I know this is true, will you please have the principal of that school call me?'

"Well," Christine continued: "two days later, the principal of that school called and offered me the job!"

"Wow! I love when that happens," I said. "How long did you teach there?"

"Twenty years."

"What grade, if I may ask?

She smiled. "First."

Christine went on to share that she was the only white person in an all-black school. Not only that, it was one of the toughest inner-city schools in Baltimore. She said it was quite a challenging place to work. The chaotic environment caused constant turnover among the staff. Even though it was an elementary school, common issues included poverty, drugs, rampant truancy, bullying and other forms of violent behavior.

Christine: One time the school hired an ex-Army drill sergeant to fill a position as a fifth-grade teacher. He lasted two months! Nobody could handle the job for long. One time I overheard a little boy telling his friend that he hated all white people. I bent down, looked him in the eye and asked: "What about me?" The little boy smiled shyly and said: "Oh, you're not white, Mrs. Miller, You're just really really light black."

After hearing such an inspiring story, I had to ask Christine what her "secret" was for surviving in her job for 20 years. When I did, her husband Ron's face lit up with pride.

Christine: (after a pause) I was known as "the lady who never raised her voice." And I never did. Every day, I just thought of each of these kids as my own, and mothered them and loved them. I never judged them. I always showed them the respect they deserved. It was easy. All I ever had to do to get them to behave was look at them.

What an inspirational story! I was so thankful to Christine for sharing it. And it's a story I would have never heard had I not been open to simply greet the person sitting next to me in a restaurant.

This beautiful "lady who never raised her voice" is but one of the millions of unsung heroes, and lovers of life and people, among us. She wasn't just a good school teacher. Christine is one of those humble, naturally kind and compassionate souls who live by the Golden Rule. Her kindness inspires respect from everyone. As a teacher, she never had to hoot and holler, rant and rave or use any form of physical discipline to get the toughest kids in the world to behave. Instead, all she needed to do was demonstrate the kind of self-respect, non-judgment and spiritual strength that, whether these little children knew it or not, they were starved for.

I felt honored to have met Christine. And what an incredible (non)coincidence, just when I'm writing a book about "Trying Softer"!

Mrs. Miller's whole life is a testament to the beauty, effectiveness, power, and joy of the "Try Softer" way. Before she was even halfway through sharing her story, I understood, with a heart filled with gratitude, how she was a gift from the Universe for me to include in this book.

My friend Beaver's "system to beat the system" was similar to the Japanese boy's plan in the parable: to hurry to his goal of becoming the ultimate karate champion. Sadly, albeit with the best of intentions, as the master in the parable teaches, it is probably the case (though we don't know for sure what caused his heart attack) that it was Beaver's extreme plan of TRYING TOO HARD that fatally overstressed his body.

Every time I think of Mr. Beaverson, I think first of his goodness. My heart then opens to the understanding and blessing that if even one person learns a lesson from his fatal choice, Beaver will not have died in vain. Likewise, every time I think of Christine, I think: Man-n-n-n...the power of "Trying Softer"!

With Deep Gratitude to Janet and Lew Klein for Contributing their Testimonial

H. Lewis Klein is a universally respected pioneer and legend in broadcasting. Beginning in the early 1950s, he produced and directed many popular TV shows. Several that baby boomers are likely to remember include *American Bandstand, Romper Room, Popeye Theater, College Press Conference, Stump the Stars, Dear Julia Mead,* and many others. He launched the careers of numerous celebrities, including Dick Clark.

The Kleins are also renowned for their contributions in academia. Lew taught fulltime at Temple University for over six decades, as well as part-time for his alma mater, the University of Pennsylvania. A visiting lecturer on several occasions, he has also lectured at the Sorbonne, University of Paris, in France. Beyond academia, Mr. Klein served the community in many ways, including producing the Philadelphia Phillies' telecasts for 15 years.

To list all of the awards and accolades Lew and Janet Klein have received in recognition of the countless ways they have helped others, through entertainment, education, and just plain philanthropic caring, I'd need to write another book. They are both exceptional human beings, with the biggest hearts. I humbly thank them for honoring me with their combined encouragement and support.

Epilogue

Thank you for sharing my "Try Softer" journey. I'm truly honored that you invested your time and attention. I trust that something in this book has touched your heart.

I hope you will agree that now is the perfect time, for all of us, to slow down, center ourselves, refocus, reconnect with our divine nature, breathe in life's sacred energy, and get on with the business of doing what we all came into this world to do:

To learn how to love and be loved.

Speaking of which...

Before I could get this book published, my dear friend Judy passed away from cancer. She was 63. I could never have written this book had she not taught me, finally, how to love and be loved. Clearly, with divine intervention, she took me to a level of self-acceptance I didn't even know existed.

From that fateful day she found out from Bonnie that I was studying *Gene Keys* and "Heart IQ," —just like her knock, knock, knock on my studio door (and my initial embarrassment) — to our blossoming friendship and my subsequent nine hours of healing tears... to our growing love and the sharing of our daily lives, I was continuously inspired to release any last remnants of blocks I had to letting love flow through my being.

Over time, Judy enabled me to relax fully into Mind/ Body/Spirit alignment, not because of any of the books we were reading, or methods of counseling we studied. Instead, she helped me become my authentic self by being such a beautiful, self-actualized human being herself. She made it practically impossible for me to maintain any blocks against any truth within me.

As time passed, our hearts blossomed for each other. We always thought it was a kind of extra joy that we both were conscious of the whole dance, as it was happening. Wow! What greater gift can you give someone than the gift of themselves?

I didn't consciously think of it before, but I realize now, as I'm typing this, that her gentle spirit gave me the final inspiration and confidence to write this book. Thankfully, Judy lived long enough to hear all of the stories in these pages. She even reviewed some parts of the manuscript. She was so excited about the prospect of the book helping others.

In the end, she faced death just as she faced life — fearlessly — with a totally open heart, mind, and soul. And never without a loving smile for everyone she met.

IN MEMORY OF
Judy Alban
(1955 – 2018)

As she smiled, danced, played her drum and revealed her beautiful soul, I gradually found the courage and strength to accept my most authentic self.

Thank you again for journeying with me. I am very honored.

ACKNOWLEDGMENTS

As easily as breathing, my heartfelt gratitude flows to my family and friends for your unwavering support of this project. Deep appreciation to Michael Wiles for not only providing this beautiful cover photo, but also for the many other wonderful images he keeps giving me to be turned into paintings. Special thanks to Brian, Laura , Lorraine , Kate, Melissa, Hilda, Sara, Summer and Dr. Peebles. Deepest gratitude as well to Michael Bernard Beckwith, Anita Rehker, all my friends at AGAPE, and Lew and Janet Klein. Especially now, after the fact, I greatly appreciate (along with the irony) all the ways and times so many of you had to remind me to "Try Softer" while writing this book. Which is to say, just relax and allow it to come through me.

Eternal thanks to my editor, Carole Greene, and publisher, Joe Clark, for enabling me to put "Try Softer" into your hands.

The book you are holding would not exist if not for the staff, the kids and the animals of Leg Up Farm. The loving energy of such a healing place and purpose is the wind beneath my Watercolor Wings.

Blessings,
Tom

We hope that you thoroughly enjoyed Tom Newnam's book, *Try Softer*. We invite you to check out our website to look through the other fine offerings from BluewaterPress LLC. Please visit us at www.bluewaterpress.com.